Decision Networks

Decision Networks

N. A. J. HASTINGS
Monash University, Melbourne, Australia

and

J. M. C. MELLO
*National Council for Scientific and Technological
Development, Rio de Janeiro*

A Wiley–Interscience Publication

JOHN WILEY & SONS
Chichester · New York · Brisbane · Toronto

Copyright © 1978, by John Wiley & Sons, Ltd.
All rights reserved.
No part of this book may be reproduced by any means, nor
translated, nor transmitted into a machine language without the written permission of the publisher.

Library of Congress Cataloging in Publication Data:

Hastings, N. A. J. 1937–
Decision networks.
'A Wiley–Interscience publication.'
1. Decision-making. 2. Industrial management.
3. Statistical decision. I. Mello, J. M. C., joint
author. II. Title.

HD30.23.H37   658.4′03   77–7336

ISBN 0 471 99531 2

Text set in 11/12 pt Photon Times,
printed by photolithography, and bound in Great Britain at
The Pitman Press, Bath

Contents

Preface

The decision network method presented in this book is a scientific aid to management decision making. It relies on the use of diagrams and a calculation procedure which are closely akin to those used in the critical path method.

A decision network is a planning model for a system. It consists of circles which represent states of the system and arrows which represent actions available to management. A path through the network represents a feasible operating plan or policy. The network is a powerful aid in clarifying the alternatives available to management and provides a logical framework for discussion and qualitative evaluation of alternative plans.

The decision network provides a visual framework to which practical management planning can be related. A simple calculation procedure almost identical to that used in critical path analysis enables individual plans to be costed and indicates the sequence of actions which maximizes profits or minimizes costs. Cash flows along the preferred or other paths are readily calculated. The second best, third best actions, etc. can also be determined for each state of the system as an additional planning aid. The computational procedure is suited to hand or computer calculation.

Decision networks have a very wide range of applications. In this respect they differ from critical path networks which relate specifically to project scheduling. The range of applications makes it difficult to give a simple but complete answer to the question, 'What can decision networks be used for?' Some examples of application areas are as follows:

    (i) Capacity planning for industrial production, public utilities and transport fleets.

    (ii) Workforce and manpower planning.

    (iii) Budget allocation.

    (iv) Product development and marketing.

    (v) Replacement policies for vehicles and equipment.

    (vi) Process planning and routeing.

    (vii) Production scheduling and stock control.

    (viii) Trimloss reduction and product standardization.

By working through a few simple examples the user becomes familiar with the principles of the technique and can then apply them to real problems. In this way the user will soon understand the capabilities and limitations of specific networks.

The technique extends into the area of probabilistic modelling where it provides a more general and at the same time a more compact approach than decision trees. Markov decision processes also feature as an important class of decision network problems. Readers familiar with dynamic programming will recognize the decision network as a form of discrete dynamic program. The algebra of dynamic programming is used in the book to provide a summary of the computational methods used, and to link with texts and reports of dynamic programming applications. *The decision network method combines the power of dynamic programming with the simplicity of critical path analysis.*

In Chapter 1 the components of a decision network are introduced with the aid of a shortest-path problem. In Chapter 2 the techniques of network formulation are developed with the aid of an example relating to the buying, selling and storing of a commodity in a warehouse. Cash flows are calculated and variations from the theoretically optimal plan are considered in a practical context. In Chapter 3 discounted cash flow is introduced in a decision network context and is illustrated by an example of production capacity planning. In Chapter 4 further applications to workforce planning, vehicle fleet capacity planning and machine replacement are illustrated. Chapter 5 is concerned with allocation problems and includes examples of an advertising budget, electricity generating and filling transport containers. Progressive networks are introduced in Chapter 6 and their application to routeing and a problem of purchasing steel bar to benefit from quantity discounts without suffering consequent trimloss is illustrated. In Chapter 7 a steel rolling/extrusion problem is considered and applications in aggregate production planning and activity sequencing to minimize resource costs are discussed.

The discussion of probabilistic models starts in Chapter 8 where the components of stochastic decision networks are introduced with the aid of a marketing problem. In Chapter 9 dynamic stock control is considered. The decision network method provides a basis for calculating re-order quantities and safety stocks for any variable pattern of demand. Chapter 10 introduces Markov decision problems and shows how these can be represented as decision networks and solved by use of an iterative calculation procedure. Chapter 11 introduces the repair limit replacement method which is a major practical application of the techniques developed in Chapter 10. In Chapters 12 and 13 discounted returns and continuous time are introduced and illustrated in the context of the repair limit replacement technique. The book concludes with a discussion of computation methods including a summary of the Dynacode package and finally a summary of applications.

In Chapters 1 to 7 only simple arithmetic is used. Algebraic summaries are given at the ends of some chapters, primarily as a link with the dynamic programming operational research technique. From Chapter 8 onwards use is made of elementary probability theory. Some calculus is used in deriving formulae for the repair limit replacement method but this is incidental to the decision network technique. The network diagrams in the manuscript version were drawn with the aid of Linex stencil number 1174.

We would like to express our appreciation to our families and colleagues who have tolerated our egocentricities during the development of this material and to Jo Baxter who typed the manuscript.

N. A. J. HASTINGS
J. M. C. MELLO

1977

CHAPTER 1

Network Components and the Shortest-path Problem

1.1 Introduction

The decision network method is a technique for the graphical representation and numerical solution of problems which involve a sequence of decisions. It is similar in style to the critical path method (PERT) in that diagrams consisting of circles and arrows are used in conjunction with a simple calculation procedure as an aid to management decision making. In its logical structure the technique is related to dynamic programming and decision trees. Network diagrams have been used to varying extents by many writers on these topics. The decision network method formalizes this approach and provides a completely developed, network based treatment for sequential decision processes.

A decision network is a planning model for a system. It consists of circles which represent states of the system and arrows which represent actions. In deterministic networks, actions are represented by single arrows. In stochastic networks, additional arrows are used to represent probabilistic transitions. A sequence of actions forms a feasible operating policy or plan. The network is a powerful aid in clarifying the alternatives available to the decision maker, and provides a logical basis for discussion and management evaluation, as well as yielding specific numerical results. The arithmetic of the method involves only addition, and in some cases multiplication. It is well suited to hand or digital computer calculations.

Decision networks have a very wide range of application. In this they differ from critical path networks which relate specifically to project scheduling. The range of applications makes it difficult to give a simple answer to the question, 'What are decision networks for?' The list of applications includes production planning, stock control, manpower planning, trimloss, replacement, capacity planning, resource allocation and so on, but this list in itself gives no idea just how the technique is used in these areas, nor of the capabilities and limitations of specific models. It is only by working through some simple examples that the user can become familiar with the principles of the technique and can then apply them to real problems.

1

In the remainder of this chapter the components of decision networks are introduced and the calculation procedure is described with the aid of a shortest-path example.

1.2 The Components of a Decision Network

State and Action

A decision network is a planning model for a system. It consists of circles which represent *states* of the system and arrows which represent *actions* by which the system is controlled or influenced. The arrows pass through a square or rectangle

Figure 1.1 Circles are states, arrows
are actions, rectangles label the actions

which contains the action label. These basic components are shown in Figure 1.1. The action arrow leads from a present state to an *adjacent state*.

A state with three actions which lead to different adjacent states is shown in Figure 1.2. This figure is a section of a network relating to a production planning

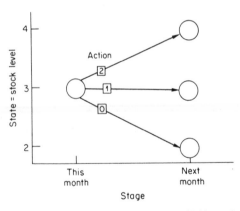

Figure 1.2 A state with three available actions

problem. The present state represents a stock level of three items at the start of the current month. One item is to be delivered to a customer from stock during the month. A decision is to be made at the start of the month to manufacture zero, one or two items during the month. The three arrows represent these three possible actions. The adjacent states represent stock levels of 2, 3 or 4 items at the start of next month. The actual choice made in practice would depend on data which is not illustrated and which does not concern us at present. Figure 1.2 illustrates in principle how we represent the situation in terms of the states and actions of a decision network.

The Markov Property

The states in a decision network must have the *Markov property*. That is, the future behaviour of the system must be independent of *how* the present state was reached. The name derives from the Russian mathematician A. A. Markov who, in the early years of the 20th century, studied a group of mathematical processes to which this property applies.

In the illustration of Figure 1.2 the Markov property means that the production decision this month may depend on the stock level at the start of the month, but must not depend on the detailed sequence of states which led to that stock level. That is it must not depend on the precise combination of production and delivery quantities, and hence the precise sequence of stock levels, which led to the stock level of three items at the start of this month. It is just the current stock level which counts.

The assumption that the Markov property holds is often close to reality. Furthermore, the same assumption is implicit in virtually all analytical techniques of management science.

The Action Set

The three arrows in Figure 1.2 represent the complete set of actions available to the decision maker in the present state, and these actions are mutually exclusive. On reaching the present state one and only one of the actions is implemented. In this respect decision networks differ from critical path networks where the arrows represent activities which must all be completed.

Returns

A return is a profit, cost, distance, time, utility, consumption or yield of a resource, etc., associated with a particular action at a given state. The return is written against the arrow which represents the corresponding action. In deterministic networks it usually appears to the right of the box containing the action label. In stochastic networks, which are considered in later chapters, the return

Figure 1.3   Action 1 gives a return of
7·2 units

appears to the left of the action label and the transition probabilities appear to the right. Figure 1.3 illustrates an action, labelled action 1, which gives a return of 7·2 units.

Stage, State, and Action Variables

Decision networks are drawn within a horizontal and vertical co-ordinate system by which the states are referenced. The variable on the horizontal axis is the *stage variable* and the variable on the vertical axis is the *state variable*. The stage variable measures progress in time or in terms of some other quantity such as the number of products to which a resource has been allocated, the number of rolling stands a steel bar has passed, and so on. The state variable represents something like a stock level, the age of a machine, the thickness of a metal sheet, the amount remaining of a resource, the current level of sales, demand, orders, etc. Integer numbers are used for the stage and state variables, emphasizing the discrete nature of the decision network model.

Actions are also labelled by an integer number which is the *action variable*. An action is something which can be done at a given state. Examples are to produce a certain amount of goods, to allocate a certain quantity of a resource, to repair a machine, to replace a machine by a new one. Note the distinction between a *decision*, which means *choosing* an action, and the action itself.

The use of the concepts of stage, state, action, and return enables us to identify common themes and structures in a wide range of practical management situations. In the decision network technique we indicate these links by including the interpretation of the stage, state, action, and return variables within the

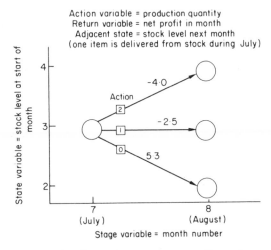

Figure 1.4   Illustrating stage, state, action, return, and adjacent state variables

network diagram. This is illustrated in Figure 1.4, which is similar to Figure 1.2 but includes the interpretation of the variables just described.

1.3 Shortest-Path Problem

The simplest type of problem to which the decision network method can be applied is finding the shortest path through a sequential network. Figure 1.5

shows an example. The problem is to find the shortest path from the initial state to the terminal state. The action variables (numbers in the boxes) label the arrows

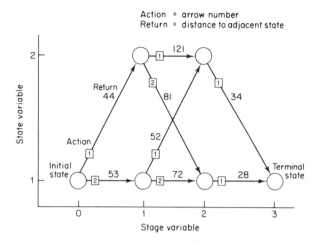

Figure 1.5   Shortest-path problem

from each state. The returns (numbers by the arrows) represent distance to the adjacent state.

Initial and Terminal States

An *initial state* of a network is a state with no input arrows. A *terminal state* is a state with no output arrows. Decision networks may have several initial and several terminal states and examples illustrating this will occur later.

Stagewise Structure

In problems with a stagewise structure every path through the network has the same number of transitions or stages. These transitions are labelled by the stage variable which appears on the horizontal axis. The decision network method can also be applied to networks which do not have a stagewise structure, provided that the network is *progressive* in the sense that no sequence of actions can lead back to a state which has already been visited. Progressive problems are considered in detail in a later chapter. The stagewise structure is more common than the progressive structure.

1.4 Calculations Directly on the Network

The calculation procedure involves a backward and a forward pass through the network. At the backward pass the shortest distance from each state to the terminal state and the best immediate choice of action at each state are determined.

In the forward pass we link a sequence of optimal actions and find the optimal path. We shall describe the calculation procedure first by working directly on the network, then in a tabular format and finally as computer input and output.

Backward Pass

The computation method involves the idea of the *value* of a state. In the shortest-path problem the value of a state is shortest distance from that state to the terminal state. We compute these values and write them in the nodes. The value of

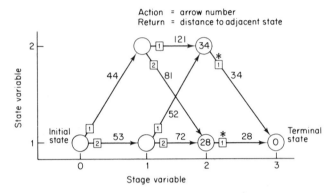

Figure 1.6   Shortest-path problem: the network after stage 2 at the backward pass

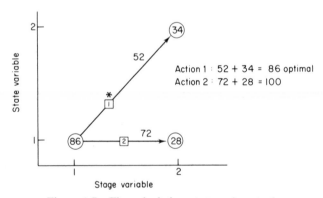

Figure 1.7   The calculation at stage 1, state 1

the terminal state is zero. The value of state 1 at stage 2 is 28 and the value of state 2 at stage 2 is 34. These are simply the direct distances to the terminal state in each case.

The optimal action at a state is the best immediate choice of direction given that we are at that state. We indicate it by putting an asterisk by its label. At stage 2, state 1 in the example the only possible action is to go directly to the terminal state and this is therefore optimal. A similar consideration applies at stage 2, state 2. At this point in the calculation the network is marked as shown in Figure 1.6.

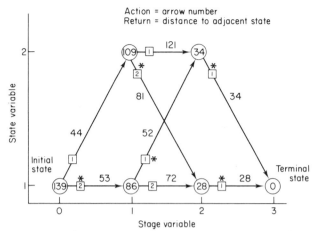

Figure 1.8 Shortest-path problem on completion of the backward pass: asterisks indicate optimal actions; the value of a state is the shortest remaining distance

We calculate the value of state 1 at stage 1 by adding the distance associated with each action to the value of the corresponding adjacent state and picking the smallest total. We find that action 1 gives $52 + 34 = 86$ and action 2 gives $72 + 28 = 100$. Action 1 has the smaller total distance and is optimal. Figure 1.7 illustrates this step. Similarly at state 2 at stage 1 we find that the value is 109 and action 2 is optimal. Finally at state 1, stage 0 (the initial state) the value is 139 and action 2 is optimal. This completes the backward pass and the network is now marked as shown in Figure 1.8.

Forward Pass

The forward pass starts at the initial state, that is stage 0, state 1. The optimizing action is selected and its arrow marked with a second asterisk. This indicates that

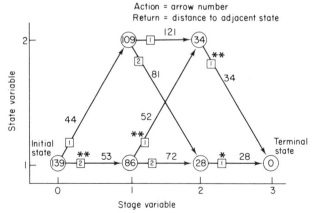

Figure 1.9 Shortest-path problem: the completed decision network

it lies on the optimal path. We then move along this arrow to the adjacent state which is stage 1, state 1. There, again we mark a second asterisk by the optimizing action and move forward along that arrow, in this case to stage 2, state 2. We continue with this procedure until a terminal state is reached. In the shortest-path problem one more step brings us to the terminal state. The double asterisks then indicate the optimal path, which in this case is: stage 0, state 1; stage 1, state 1; stage 2, state 2; stage 3, state 1. The value of the initial state, in this case 139, is the length of the shortest path. The calculation also yields the shortest distance from every state to the terminal state and the optimizing actions at every state. The final form of the decision network is shown in Figure 1.9.

1.5 Tabular Method for Hand Calculations

Network representation is ideal for illustrating the formulation of a problem and for calculating small networks. For larger networks and particularly those with repetitive data there are advantages in using a tabular method. Similar data tables can be used for either hand calculation or for computer input using the Dynacode computer package, further details of which are given in Appendix A. The hand calculation method is described in this section and the computer input and output are discussed in Section 1.6.

The tabular calculations for the shortest-path problem are shown in Table 1.1. Table 1.2 summarizes the role of each column in Table 1.1. Table 1.3 gives the optimal path. The detailed development of Table 1.1 is as follows.

Backward Pass

The calculation table is developed in the same sequence as is used in the backward pass of the network based calculation. We start by entering details of the terminal

Table 1.1 Shortest-path problem: calculations in tabular format. Each of rows 2 to 9 contains data and calculations relating to one action

Column	1	2	3	4	5	6	7
Row	Stage	State	Action	Return	Adjacent state	Trial value	Rank
1	3	1				0	(terminal state
2	2	1	1	28	1	28 + 0 = 28	1*
3	2	2	1	34	1	34 + 0 = 34	1**
4	1	1	1	52	2	52 + 34 = 86	1**
5	1	1	2	72	1	72 + 28 = 100	2
6	1	2	1	121	2	121 + 34 = 155	2
7	1	2	2	81	1	81 + 28 = 109	1*
8	0	1	1	44	2	44 + 109 = 153	2
9	0	1	2	53	1	53 + 86 = 139	1**

state or states. In the shortest-path problem there is only one terminal state. This is state 1 at stage 3 and it has value 0. Row 1 of Table 1.1 shows the entry we make for this. The stage and state variables are entered in columns 1 and 2 respectively and the value is entered in column 6. The other columns of the terminal state row are left blank in the hand calculation method.

We now continue with the backward pass and move to stage 2. It does not matter in what order we consider the states at a given stage but we must complete the analysis of each state before we move on to the next and we must complete the analysis of all the states at a given stage before we move to the next.

Row 2 of Table 1.1 relates to stage 2, state 1, action 1. The distance to the adjacent state is 2 units and so the entry 2 appears in the 'Return' column, column 4. The adjacent state is state 1 (by implication this is state 1 at stage 3). The trial value is the remaining distance when the current action is used and an optimal plan is used from the adjacent state. This is $28 + 0 = 28$. Since this is the only action at this state it is necessarily the best. We indicate this by entering 1 in the rank column. A star is also added as this makes it easier to identify the optimal actions and values, and links in with the system used when the calculations are done on the network. This concludes the entry for stage 2, state 1. The entry for stage 2, state 2 is derived similarly and is shown in row 3 of Table 1.1. The double star in column 7 of row 3 is a result of the forward pass and does not appear at this point in the calculations. The entries for stage 2 are now concluded.

The entries for stage 1, state 1 appear in rows 4 and 5. Row 4 contains the entry for action 1. The return or distance is 5 units and the arrow leads to state 2 at stage 2. The value of state 2 at stage 2 is obtained from row 3, column 6, and is 3. The trial value is therefore given by $52 + 34 = 86$. At this point we cannot complete the rank column because we have not yet evaluated action 2. We therefore proceed with row 5. The return is 72, the adjacent state is state 1 whose value, obtained from row 2, is 28. The trial value is $72 + 28 = 100$. This completes the action set at stage 1, state 1 and we can now rank the actions.

In order to find the shortest path through the network it is only necessary to find the best action at each state, that is the action of rank 1. However, in management applications the decision network may not be an exact model of the true

Table 1.2   Explanation of the use of columns in Table 1.1 (rows 2 to 9)

Column 1	The stage variable of the start node of an action
Column 2	The state variable of the start node of the action
Column 3	The action variable of the action
Column 4	The return associated with the action
Column 5	The adjacent state variable, that is the state variable of the end node of the action arrow
Column 6	The 'trial value' of action, obtained by adding its return to the (optimal) value of its adjacent state
Column 7	The 'rank' of the action. The optimal action at a state has rank 1, the second best action has rank 2 and so on. Optimal actions are also indicated by a star and actions on the optimal path by a double star

situation and the additional information provided by knowing the second best and third best actions, etc., can often be useful. We therefore illustrate a procedure for finding these, which is simply by sorting the trial values in order of size. In a minimization problem the smallest trial value indicates the best action which has rank 1, the second smallest trial value indicates the second best action which has rank 2 and so on. At the present point in the calculation action 1 has rank 1 and action 2 has rank 2. These ranks are entered in column 7, rows 4 and 5. The best action is highlighted by adding a star. The second star in row 4 is entered at the forward pass.

Continuing with state 2 at stage 1 the entries in rows 6 and 7 are made. Action 2 is optimal and is accorded rank 1.

Finally, we move to stage 0 where rows 8 and 9 show the calculation. Action 2 is optimal and gives the value 139.

Forward Pass

At the forward pass we work up the table, starting from the initial state which will be at or near the bottom. In Table 1.1 rows 8 and 9 relate to the initial state. We look at the rank column of these rows and identify the optimal action. This is action 2, indicated by rank 1 and a star in row 9, column 7. We add a second star to column 7 of this row indicating that this state is on the optimal path. We now look at column 5 of this row (row 9) to find the adjacent state. This is state 1. We move up the table to the next stage and find the block of rows relating to state 1, in this case rows 4 and 5.

We examine the rank column of this block and find the row which is rank 1. We add a second star to column 7 of this row, in this case row 4. We then again identify the adjacent state, which from column 5 of row 4 we see is state 2. We move up the table again, in this case to row 3 which is the only row for state 2 at stage 2. We add a second star to column 7 and identify the adjacent state from column 5. Moving to the adjacent state, state 1 at stage 3, we find that it is a terminal state. The forward pass is therefore finished, and the double asterisks indicate the rows which contain the optimal sequence of actions.

Finally, we can express the result as in Table 1.3. The rows in this table correspond to the double asterisk rows in Table 1.1, but are listed in a forward sequence

Table 1.3   Shortest-path problem: tabular format for the optimal path

Row	Stage	State	Action	Value
1	0	1	2	139
2	1	1	1	86
3	2	2	1	34
4	3	1	0	0

and omit some detail. Rows 1, 2, 3, 4 of Table 1.3 correspond to rows 9, 4, 3, 1 of Table 1.1 respectively.

1.6 Using a Computer

Decision network calculations are well suited to the use of a digital computer. Special programs can be written for particular applications or use made of a package such as Dynacode, which provides for a wide range of decision network calculations, including deterministic stochastic, progressive, discounted, infinite stage, and semi-Markov problems. A summary of this system is given in Chapter 14. The Dynacode input and output for the shortest-path problem are shown in Figure 1.10 and Table 1.4 respectively. The input consists of several Dynacode

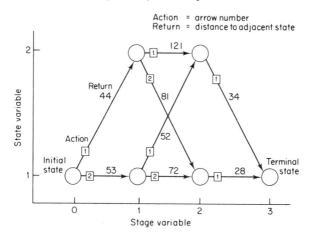

Input	Statement number
DYNACODE SHORTEST-PATH PROBLEM	1
LIST INPUT	2
MINIMIZE	3
TERMINAL STATES I	4
* VALUE IS SHORTEST DISTANCE TO TERMINAL STATE	5
DATA	6

stage	state	action	value or return	adjacent state - not punched	Statement number
3	1	0	0	0 — terminal state	7
2	1	1	28	1	8
2	2	1	34	1 — one row per	9
1	1	1	52	2 — arrow in	10
1	1	2	72	1 — backward	11
1	2	1	121	2 — pass	12
1	2	2	81	1 — sequence	13
0	1	1	44	2	14
0	1	2	53	1	15
END					16

Figure 1.10   Shortest-path problem and Dynacode input

program statements (these will usually be preceded by job control statements which are special to the installation used) followed by the problem data in an appropriate sequence. The output appears automatically in a standard format, subject to some controls by the user.

Figure 1.10 shows the shortest-path problem and its Dynacode input. Statements 1 to 6 are program statements. Statement 1 consists of the word

DYNACODE followed by any alphanumeric characters specified by the user. This statement acts as the title of the program and is also printed as the first line of the output. Statement 2 is LIST INPUT. This causes the input to be listed; if it is omitted the input is not listed. Statement 3, MINIMIZE, indicates a minimization problem (shortest path). If it were omitted a maximization problem (longest path) would be assumed. Statement 4 specifies the number of terminal states, in this case 1. Statement 5 illustrates a comment which is any statement starting with an asterisk. Comments can contain any alphanumeric entries and are printed on the output where they precede the numerical results. They are mainly used to summarize the problem formulation. Statement 6, DATA, announces the start of the data.

The data consist of rows of numbers. Each row always contains five numbers, and at certain points dummy entries (usually zeros) are used to ensure that five numbers always appear. The numbers are in free format, separated by one or more blanks or by commas. There is a row of data for each terminal state, followed by a row for each arrow in the decision network. The sequence of the data is important and must be the same as in the tabular format of the backward pass calculations.

The first row of data (statement 7, Figure 1.10) relates to the terminal state. The five entries include two dummies and are as follows:

(i) The stage variable of the terminal stage (integer).
(ii) The state variable of the terminal state (integer).
(iii) A dummy entry, usually zero.
(iv) The value of the terminal state (integer or real). In the example the value happens to be zero.
(v) A dummy entry, usually zero.

The use of zero as a dummy entry does *not* preclude the use of zero as a stage, state, action or return variable.

The remaining data consist of one row for each arrow in the network, in the same sequence as the arrows are processed in the backward pass calculation. That is the data for stage 2 comes next, with all the actions at a given state appearing in adjacent rows, then the data at stage 1 and finally stage 0.

For each arrow in the decision network the corresponding data statement consists of the following five entries:

(i) The stage variable of the start node (integer).
(ii) The state variable of the start node (integer).
(iii) The action variable (integer).
(iv) The return (integer or real).
(v) The state variable of the end node (integer). This is referred to as the adjacent state.

Figure 1.11 illustrates in detail the correspondence between a decision network arrow and its Dynacode data.

The stage, state, and action variables must be integers in the range −9999 to

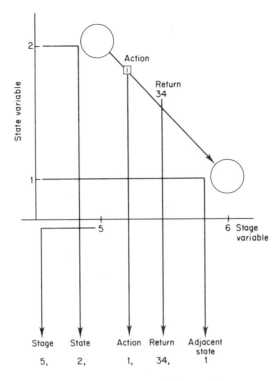

Figure 1.11   Decision arrow and Dynacode statement

9999 (zero is allowed). The return variable can be real or integer but must not exceed eleven characters in length including minus sign and decimal point if any.

Comparing the Dynacode data with the tabular method of calculation we see that the data are the same as columns 1 to 5 of Table 1.1 but with zeros rather than blanks appearing in the terminal state row.

The output is shown in Table 1.4. This is similar to Table 1.3 and gives the optimal path in a tabular format. If the statement RANK k is included in the

Table 1.4   Dynacode output for the shortest-path problem

DYNACODE SHORTEST PATH PROBLEM
*VALUE IS SHORTEST DISTANCE TO
TERMINAL STATE OPTIMAL PROCESS

Stage	State	Action	Value
0	1	2	139·0
1	1	1	86·0
2	2	1	34·0
3	1	0	0·0

Dynacode program, where k is a positive integer, an additional table will be printed showing the k best actions at each state. Thus information equivalent to the full results of Table 1.1 can be obtained. If a tie occurs when actions are evaluated, Dynacode gives preference to the first action found.

CHAPTER 2

Network Formulation and the Warehouse Problem

2.1 Introduction

The shortest-path problem of Chapter 1 illustrates the network components and calculations which, with some extensions, are used in all decision network applications. The remainder of the book is mainly concerned with how to formulate and apply decision networks in a variety of practical situations.

Formulating a problem as a decision network requires some skill and experience. The examples in this book illustrate the main types of application and familiarity with these will give the reader an understanding of the technique and enable him to formulate original networks.

The best approach to formulating a new problem is to consider the decision which must be made initially and to attempt to sketch this in network form. The decisions which immediately follow are then sketched and the overall form of the network becomes clear. This will often show that the problem fits into a pattern with which the user is familiar. Once the pattern of the network is established the stage, state, action, return, and adjacent state variables can be identified. The user is strongly recommended to write down the interpretation of these variables either on the network or in an accompanying table. The network and the accompanying identification of the stage, state, action, return, and adjacent state variables constitute the formulation of the problem as a decision network. Once this information is committed to paper it is self-explanatory to anyone familiar with the technique.

If the network is small the calculations can be done by hand on the network which is then used as a basis for planning, discussion, and implementation. If the network is large it is not necessary to draw it in detail. Just draw enough to illustrate the formulation and to identify the stage, state, action, return, and adjacent state variables. Then list these in the tabular format and carry out the calculations either by hand or by computer. For planning and discussion purposes it may be useful to transfer the results back into network form. The user rapidly becomes familiar with the structure of his own problem and will soon acquire a clear mental picture of its decision network.

15

We illustrate these principles by considering a problem relating to the buying, selling, and storage of a commodity whose price varies over a period of years—the warehouse problem.

2.2 The Warehouse Problem

Situation

A company owns a warehouse in which it can store a food commodity which is harvested annually.

Decisions to buy, sell or store the commodity are made on a yearly basis and relate to a five-year planning period. The decisions are based on a forecast of the buying and selling price and on the cost of storage. For simplicity we shall assume that all actions involve buying, selling, or storing the entire contents of the warehouse. Problems involving intermediate stock levels would be similar in principle.

At the beginning of each year the warehouse is either empty (state 0) or full (state 1). The following actions are available. The action variable represents the amount purchased in the current year.

Warehouse full: (state 1)	Action −1. Sell the contents and buy nothing. This leaves the warehouse empty at the start of the next year.
	Action 0. Keep the warehouse full for the year.
	Action 1. Sell the contents of the warehouse and purchase fresh stock so that the warehouse is again full at the start of the next year.
Warehouse empty: (state 0)	Action 0. Keep the warehouse empty for the year.
	Action 1. Buy sufficient to fill the warehouse.

The price of the commodity is influenced by government stockpiling policies and by the existence of some long term company contracts with producers. A forecast of the net buying and selling price of the commodity, for amounts equivalent to the entire contents of the warehouse, has been prepared, covering the five-year period 1980 to 1984. This is shown in Table 2.1.

Table 2.1 *Buying and selling prices over the five-year period 1980–4*

Year	1980	1981	1982	1983	1984
Buying price	10	12	19	15	12
Selling price	11	13	16	16	12

If the warehouse is kept full for a year with no stock movement there is a charge of 2 units; if it is kept empty a cost of 1 unit is incurred. If the warehouse is full when the end of the five-year planning period is reached the value of the contents is reckoned to be 10 units. It is now the beginning of 1980 and the warehouse is currently full.

Aim

The aim of the company as far as we are concerned is to maximize profits. Our information relates to a five-year period, but the value of any stock at the end of the period must be taken into account. Specifically, therefore, the aim is to maximize the sum of the profit in the period and value of the stock at the end of the period. If we wanted simply to maximize profit in the planning period we could do this by setting the value of any closing stock to zero.

2.3 Formulation and Network Solution

The Decision in 1980

The first decision occurs at the beginning of 1980. The warehouse is full and three actions are available. Firstly, we may sell the contents and buy nothing. In this case we get a return of 11 units which is the selling price of the commodity given in Table 2.1. Under this action the warehouse will be empty at the beginning of 1981 which is the next decision point. Secondly, we may store the contents of the warehouse with no buying or selling. This means a cost of 2 units. We shall

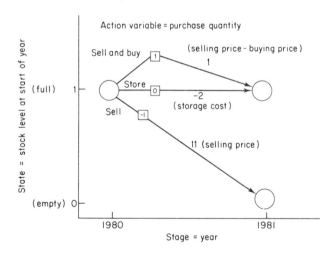

Figure 2.1   The decision in 1980: network representation

express the returns in profit terms, so this is a return of −2. Thirdly, we may sell the present contents of the warehouse for 11 units and buy fresh stock for 9 units. This yields a return of 2 units and leaves the warehouse full at the start of 1981.

The actions just described are summarized in Table 2.2. The network representation of the decision is shown in Figure 2.1. Note that parallel actions are allowed (that is, actions with the same start and end node). For ease of drawing we can bend an arrow at its action label.

Table 2.2   The decision in 1980: list of actions

Action variable	Action	Return	Adjacent state
-1	sell	$11 =$ selling price	$0 =$ empty
0	store	$-2 =$ storage cost	$1 =$ full
1	sell and buy	$1 =$ selling price buying price	$1 =$ full

The Decisions in 1981

Continuing with the formulation procedure, we consider the decision in 1981. At the start of 1981 the warehouse may be full or empty, depending on the action chosen in 1980. If it is full the decision has exactly the same form as the 1980 decision shown in Figure 2.1. The only difference will be the returns which will involve 1981 prices. If the warehouse is empty two actions are available. Firstly, we may leave the warehouse empty. This incurs a cost of 1 unit, that is a return of -1, and leads to adjacent state 0, that is an empty warehouse at the start of 1982. Secondly, we may buy sufficient to fill the warehouse. The buying price in 1981 is 12 units and since this is expenditure the return is -12. These actions are sum-

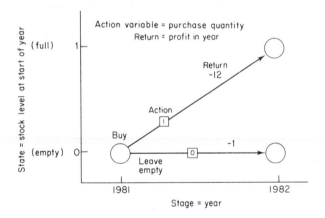

Figure 2.2   Decision in 1981 with warehouse empty

marized in Table 2.3 and the network representation of the decision is shown in Figure 2.2.

The Complete Network

The complete network is formed by linking together sections like Figures 2.1 and 2.2. The five-year planning period extends from the beginning of 1980 to the beginning of 1985 and so there are five stages. At the beginning of 1985 the warehouse may be either full or empty, so there are two terminal states. If the

Table 2.3   Decision in 1981 with warehouse empty: list of actions

Action variable	Action	Return	Adjacent state
0	leave empty	−1	0 = empty
1	buy	−12	1 = full

warehouse is full the contents have value 10 units so the value of state 1 at stage 1985 is 10. If the warehouse is empty at the beginning of 1985 we are in state 0 at

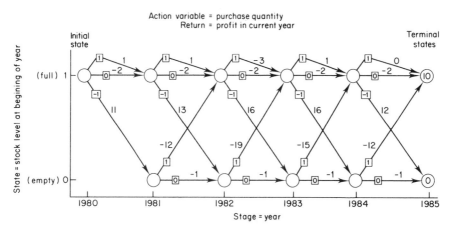

Figure 2.3   Warehouse problem: the decision network before calculation starts

stage 1985 and this has value 0. The complete decision network, before calculation commences, is shown in Figure 2.3.

The calculations follow the same method as for the shortest-path problem except that, as we wish to maximize profits, we choose the action with maximum rather than minimum total future return at each state. The decision network with complete calculations is shown in Figure 2.4. The optimal path is marked by double asterisks and involves the sequence of actions shown in Table 2.4. The maximum total profit plus value of terminal stock is 16 units. Under the optimal

Table 2.4   Warehouse problem optimal plan

Stage (year)	State (stock level)	Action	Value (future profit terminal stock value)
1980	1 = full	1 = sell and buy	16
1981	1 = full	1 = sell and buy	15
1982	1 = full	−1 = sell	14
1983	0 = empty	0 = leave empty	−2
1984	0 = empty	1 = leave empty	−1
1985	0 = empty		0

20

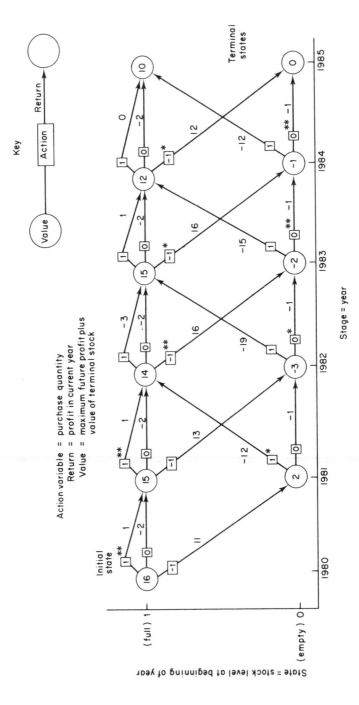

Figure 2.4. Warehouse problem: the decision network when the calculation is complete. Asterisks indicate optimal actions; double asterisks indicate the optimal path

plan the stock level at the beginning of 1985 will be zero, so, as it turns out, a total profit of 16 units is actually generated within the five-year period.

2.4 Discussion

Table 2.4 gives the mathematically optimal solution to the warehouse problem with the data as stated. In practice the data may be uncertain and the choice of planning period and terminal values may be open to doubt. The decision network provides a framework for visualizing and assessing these uncertainties. If the optimal plan differs significantly from our expectations then either our estimates of the cost data or our intuitive interpretation of the implications of these data needs revision.

Alternative planning periods, alternative terminal values, and alternative assessments of the buying and selling prices can be evaluated by modifying the data and repeating the calculations. This sensitivity analysis is greatly assisted by the use of a computer.

We may also wish to bring in discounting of future returns. One way to do this is by expressing the returns (and terminal values) in terms of present values. An alternative method in which the values are expressed as present values related to the time of the current action can also be used and this is described in Chapter 3. If Dynacode is used, discounting is allowed for very simply by inserting a statement in the program which specifies the interest rate as a percentage. The data themselves are left in undiscounted form and all necessary adjustment for discounting is carried out by the package.

Cash Flow

Several subsidiary results can be read from the decision network. One of these is the cash flow over the planning period for the optimal plan, or indeed any plan. The cash flows in the years (on a year by year basis) are given by the returns, which appear on the networks. For example, for the optimal plan indicated by

Table 2.5   Cash flow

Year	Cash flow	
	Current	Cumulative
1980	1	1
1981	1	2
1982	16	18
1983	−1	17
1984	−1	16

double asterisks in Figure 2.4 the cash flows in years 1980 to 1984 are as shown in Table 2.5.

Near-Optimal Analysis

As well as giving the optimal path, the decision network shows the best actions at states not on this path. If we find that we are forced off the optimal path we still have a sequence of optimizing actions to follow. This will not always mean a return to the original optimal path. The loss of profit associated with taking a non-optimal action can be calculated. Referring to Figure 2.4 consider state 1 at stage 1980. The optimal action is action 1 which gives a return of 1 unit in the current year and, if an optimal plan is used thereafter, the future profit is 15 units. Thus the optimal value of 16 units is obtained. However, suppose that there are certain benefits to be derived from selling the contents of the warehouse so that it is empty at the start of 1981. For example, we may be able to let the warehouse for one year at a profit of 4 units. Is this worthwhile? From the decision network the return this year from selling the contents is 11 units and this action takes us to state 0 at stage 1981. From there the maximum profit is 2 units. Hence the total profit from the commodity would be $11 + 2 = 13$ units. Adding the letting profit of 4 units gives a total of 17 and makes this action attractive.

2.5 Tabular Calculations and Computer Method

The warehouse problem can be solved using the tabular calculation method

Table 2.6   Warehouse problem: hand calculations in tabular format

Column	1	2	3	4	5	6	7
Row	Stage	State	Action	Return	Adjacent state	Trial value	Rank
1	1985	0	0	0	0	0 ⎰ terminal	
2	1985	1	0	10	0	10 ⎱ states	
3	1984	0	0	−1	0	$-1 + 0 = -1$	1**
4	1984	0	1	−12	1	$-12 + 10 = -2$	2
5	1984	1	−1	12	0	$12 + 0 = 12$	1*
6	1984	1	0	−2	1	$-2 + 10 = 8$	3
7	1984	1	1	0	1	$0 + 10 = 10$	2
8	1983	0	0	−1	0	$-1 - 1 = -2$	1**
9	1983	0	1	−15	1	$-15 + 12 = -3$	2
10	1983	1	−1	16	0	$16 - 1 = 15$	1*
11	1983	1	0	−2	1	$-2 + 12 = 10$	3
12	1983	1	1	1	1	$1 + 12 = 13$	2
13	1982	0	0	−1	0	$-1 - 2 = -3$	1*
14	1982	0	1	−19	1	$-19 + 15 = -4$	2
15	1982	1	−1	16	0	$16 - 2 = 14$	1**
16	1982	1	0	−2	1	$-2 + 15 = 13$	2
17	1982	1	1	−3	1	$-3 + 15 = 12$	3
18	1981	0	0	−1	0	$-1 - 3 = -4$	2
19	1981	0	1	−12	1	$-12 + 14 = 2$	1*
20	1981	1	−1	13	0	$13 - 3 = 10$	3
21	1981	1	0	−2	1	$-2 + 14 = 12$	2
22	1981	1	1	1	1	$1 + 14 = 15$	1**
23	1980	1	−1	11	0	$11 + 2 = 13$	2
24	1980	1	0	−2	1	$-2 + 15 = 13$	3
25	1980	1	1	1	1	$1 + 15 = 16$	1**

described in Chapter 1, Section 1.6 and Table 1.1. The full hand calculations are shown in Table 2.6. The computer input and output for this problem using Dynacode are shown in Tables 2.7(a) and 2.7(b).

Table 2.7(a)   Warehouse problem: Dynacode input

```
DYNACODE WAREHOUSE PROBLEM - DECISION NETWORKS
LIST INPUT
TERMINAL STATES 2
RANK 2
*STAGE IS YEAR
*STATE 1 = FULL FOR WHICH:
   *ACTION -1 = SELL
   *ACTION  0 = STORE
   *ACTION  1 = SELL AND BUY
*STATE 2 = EMPTY FOR WHICH:
   *ACTION  0 = LEAVE EMPTY
   *ACTION  1 = BUY
*VALUE = PROFIT IN PLANNING PERIOD PLUS VALUE OF TERMINAL STOCK
DATA
1985,0,0,0,0
1985,1,1,10,0
1984,0,0,-1,0
1984,0,1,-12,1
1984,1,-1,12,0
1984,1,0,-2,1
1984,1,1,0,1
1983,0,0,-1,0
1983,0,1,-15,1
1983,1,-1,16,0
1983,1,0,-2,1
1983,1,1,1,1
1982,0,0,-1,0
1982,0,1,-19,1
1982,1,-1,16,0
1982,1,0,-2,1
1982,1,1,-3,1
1981,0,0,-1,0
1981,0,1,-12,1
1981,1,-1,13,0
1981,1,0,-2,1
1981,1,1,1,1
1980,1,-1,11,0
1980,1,0,-2,1
1980,1,1,1,1
END
```

The Data are the same as columns 1 to 5 of rows 1 to 25 of Table 2.6

2.6 Definitions and Algebraic Summary

The calculation procedures which we have described were originally developed by Richard Bellman (1957) on an algebraic basis. Following Bellman, we shall refer to the algebraic form of the technique as 'dynamic programming'. Dynamic programming allows (in principle) for possibly continuous variables and functions

Table 2.7(b)   Warehouse problem: Dynacode output

```
DYNACODE WAREHOUSE PROBLEM - DECISION NETWORKS
*STAGE IS YEAR
*STATE 1 = FULL FOR WHICH:
   *ACTION -1 = SELL
   *ACTION  0 = STORE
   *ACTION  1 = SELL AND BUY
*STATE 2 = EMPTY FOR WHICH:
   *ACTION  0 = LEAVE EMPTY
   *ACTION  1 = BUY
*VALUE = PROFIT IN PLANNING PERIOD PLUS VALUE OF TERMINAL STOCK
*
BEST ACTION LIST TO RANK    2
*
```

STAGE	STATE	ACTION	VALUE
1984	0	0	-1.000
1984	0	1	-2.000
1984	1	-1	12.000
1984	1	1	10.000
1983	0	0	-2.000
1983	0	1	-3.000
1983	1	-1	15.000
1983	1	1	13.000
1982	0	0	-3.000
1982	0	1	-4.000
1982	1	-1	14.000
1982	1	0	13.000
1981	0	1	2.000
1981	0	0	-4.000
1981	1	1	15.000
1981	1	0	12.000
1980	1	1	16.000
1980	1	-1	13.000

```
*
OPTIMAL PROCESS FROM INITIAL STATE    1
*
```

STAGE	STATE	ACTION	VALUE
1980	1	1	16.000
1981	1	1	15.000
1982	1	-1	14.000
1983	0	0	-2.000
1984	0	0	-1.000
1985	0	0	0.000

```
END
```

The title and comment statements are taken from the input.
The RANK 2 table gives the best and second best action at each state.
The optimal process table gives the result found in Table 2.4.

and for the use of calculus and other procedures for maximization or minimization. More subtle optimization criteria, such as maximization of the minimum return, may also be considered in either a dynamic programming or decision network contexts. We now summarize the key terms which are common to both decision networks and dynamic programming and link them to the algebraic

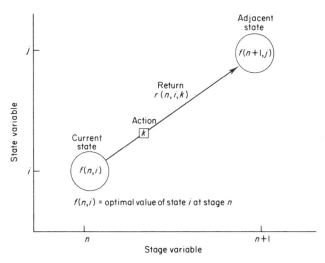

Figure 2.5 Algebraic symbols for decision network quantities

representation of the computational method. These terms and symbols also appear in Figure 2.5.

State: A state is a configuration of a system and is identified by the features or properties of that configuration.

Examples: Current position in shortest-path problem, stock level in warehouse problem, age of machine in replacement problem, current capacity in plant capacity problem.

Network symbol: A circle (node). The state variable also appears on the vertical axis of the network.

Algebraic symbol: State variable $= i$.

Stage: The decision network method is concerned with systems which undergo processes involving a sequence of transitions from one state to another. A stage is a single step in such a process and corresponds to the movement of a system from its current state to an adjacent state.

Examples: A stage is often a time interval such as a week, month or year. It may also be a physical transition such as movement to the next point on a route or movement through a process, e.g. a steel rolling stand.

Network representation: The stage variable appears on the horizontal axis of the network.

Algebraic symbol: Stage variable $= n$.

Action: An action is something which can be done at the current state. The effect of an action is to generate a return and to cause the system to move to a particular adjacent state. At each state there is a set of actions available from amongst which a choice must be made. Actions are assumed to be mutually exclusive.

Examples: Going to a particular adjacent state in a routeing problem; order quantity, production quantity, repair or replace a machine, cash allocation to current project.

Network symbol: An arrow, labelled by a rectangular box.

Algebraic symbol: Action variable $= k$.

Return:
A return is something that the system generates over one stage of a process and is dependent on the stage, state, and action.

Examples: The distance between two nodes, the profit in the current year, resource consumption in current time period, cost incurred at current stage of a process.

Network representation: The return appears as a number written near the corresponding action arrow.

Algebraic symbol: $r(n, i, k) =$ return associated with stage n, state i, action k.

Adjacent state:
The state to which the system goes next.

Network representation: The particular node to which an action arrow leads.

Algebraic symbol: Adjacent state variable $= j$. The adjacent state variable will be determined by the current stage, state and action, and the relationship between these quantities may be expressed as a transition function of the form $j = t(n, i, k)$. For example, in a stock control problem with demand $d(n)$ at stage n, stock level i and order quantity k, the transition equation would be $j = i + k - d(n)$. This corresponds to the relationship, new stock level = current stock + order quantity − demand.

Optimal value of a state:
The optimal value of a state is the maximum (minimum if minimizing) sum of the returns generated over the remaining stages of the process, including the value of the terminal state reached.

Examples: Maximum total remaining profit, minimum total remaining cost, shortest total remaining distance.

Network representation: The optimal value of each state is written in the corresponding node during the backward pass calculations.

Algebraic symbol: $f(n, i) =$ optimal value of state i at stage n.

The Dynamic Programming Recurrence Relation

The backward pass of the calculation procedure is represented by the following equation which is called the dynamic programming recurrence relation:

$$f(n, i) = \underset{k}{\text{Max}} \, [r(n, i, k) + f(n + 1, j)] \qquad (2.1)$$

The term in square brackets on the right-hand side of equation (2.1) is the sum of the return $r(n, i, k)$ under a given action k, and the value $f(n + 1, j)$ of the adjacent state j which is reached when that action is used. The next stage is assumed to be labelled $n + 1$. This term is the value of the given action, and corresponds to the sum of the number by the arrow and the number in the adjacent node. The Max operator means that the maximum overall action values is found and this is then the optimal value of the current state.

The dynamic programming recurrence relation provides a very compact summary of the calculation procedure. By itself, however, it gives the user little clue as to the physical meaning of any underlying applied process, particularly since it remains the same for all applications.

2.7 Forward Recurrence

The decision network calculation procedure in the form so far described involves firstly a backward pass at which optimal state values are calculated and then a forward pass at which the optimal path is identified. This is called the *backward recurrence* calculation method. An alternative or additional calculation procedure is *forward recurrence*. Deterministic problems without discounting or with pre-discounted returns (Section 3.3) can be solved equally well using either backward or forward recurrence.

For stochastic problems and for recursive discounting, backward recurrence must be used. The forward recurrence procedure will be illustrated by reference to the warehouse problem of Figure 2.3.

To apply the forward recurrence calculation procedure some minor modifications to the decision network formulation are required. The optimal value of a state is now defined as the maximum total profit which can be generated in reaching that state from an initial state. The initial and terminal states change roles and we must start by giving known values to the initial states. The values of the terminal states are accommodated by introducing an additional stage with one action per state, this action having a return equal to the terminal value of the corresponding old terminal state. The additional stage is referred to as an *extension stage*. Figure 2.6 shows the forward recurrence decision network for the warehouse problem before calculation starts. Comparing Figures 2.3 and 2.6 we see that in the latter the initial state has been given the value zero and the old terminal values of 10 units for state 1 and zero for state 0 have been replaced by an extension stage. The extension stage does not represent an actual time period. It is an artificial device which allows the calculation procedure to select the path which yields the greatest total profit. This path may pass through either of the states at

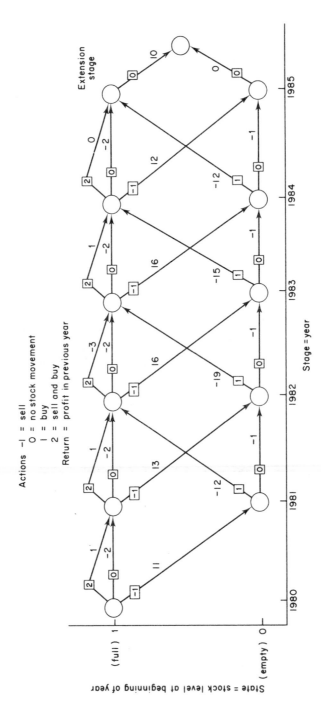

Figure 2.6   Warehouse problem: the forward recurrence decision network before calculation starts

stage 1985. The returns at the extension stage correspond to the old terminal values, whilst the action labels are arbitrary and have been entered as zeros.

The action arrows now relate to the states to which they are inputs and their start nodes are the adjacent states. Thus the current and adjacent states exchange roles, giving the situation shown in Figure 2.7.

This change in the assignment of the actions may require a new definition of the action variable. In the warehouse problem we now label the buy and sell action as

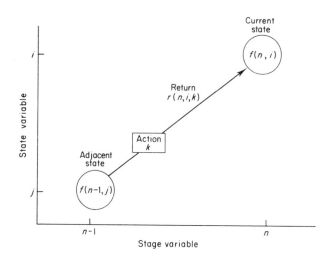

Figure 2.7   Forward recurrence: the current and adjacent states change roles when compared with backward recurrence

action 2, since otherwise states 1 would have two input arrows labelled action 1. The forward recurrence relation (compare equation (2.1)) is

$$f(n, i) = \underset{k}{\text{Max}} \; [r(n, i, k) + f(n-1, j)]. \qquad (2.2)$$

Warehouse Problem

The decision network for the warehouse problem with completed calculations is shown in Figure 2.8. The calculation starts with the assignment of the value zero to state 1 at stage 1980. Then each state at stage 1981 is considered in turn. State 0 has only one action with a return of 11 units, so the value of this state is 11 units and this action is optimal. Note that actions now relate to the states to which they act as *inputs*. In a sense, in the forward recurrence method the decisions at each state are somewhat artificial, since one is asking 'by what action should I reach this state?' Backward recurrence is more representative of the actual decision-making process in that at each state we are asking 'what action should I take now?'

30

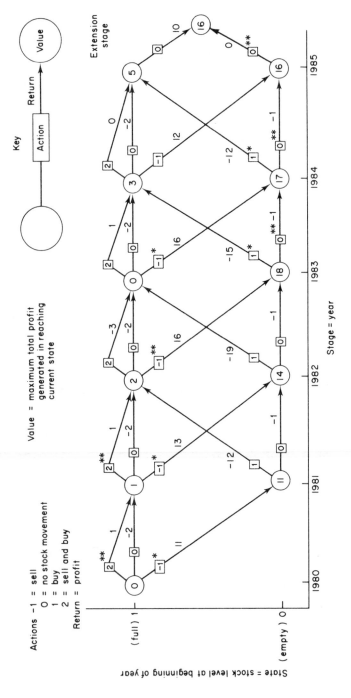

Figure 2.8   Warehouse problem with forward recurrence calculations: double asterisks indicate the optimal path; asterisks indicate optimal actions and are optimal inputs to the corresponding states

Continuing to state 1 at stage 1981, there is a choice between action 0 and action 2 as follows:

$$\text{Action 0:} \quad 0 - 2 = -2$$
$$\text{Action 2:} \quad 0 + 1 = 1$$

Action 2 is optimal and state 1 has value 1 unit.

The decision at state 0 at stage 1982 is illustrated in Figure 2.9. The calculations are as follows:

$$\text{Action} -1: \quad 1 + 13 = 14$$
$$\text{Action} 0: \quad 11 - 1 = 10$$

Action -1 is optimal and state 0 has value 14. The remaining calculations continue similarly until the forward pass is complete.

The optimal path is found in a backward pass from the extension stage. This pass is similar to the forward pass of backward recurrence. The optimal action at

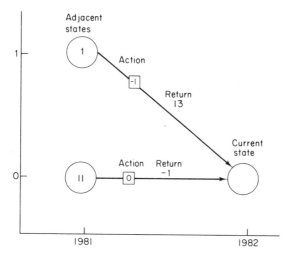

Figure 2.9   Forward recurrence solution of the warehouse
problem: the decision at state 0, stage 1982

the current state is identified and marked by a second asterisk. We then move to the adjacent state under this action and repeat the procedure. The optimal path is thus marked out by double asterisks.

The optimal path found by forward recurrence is the same as found by backward recurrence. The total value generated will also be the same. The state values otherwise will be different, since they now represent profits generated from the beginning of the planning period rather than over the remainder of the period. The actions with single asterisks will also be different. In forward recurrence they represent sequences of actions by which each state can be reached optimally, that is, at maximum profit.

32

Table 2.8(a)   Warehouse problem Dynacode input for forward recurrence

```
DYNACODE WAREHOUSE PROBLEM - FORWARD RECURRENCE FORMULATION
LIST INPUT
TERMINAL STATES 1
RANK 1
* STAGE IS YEAR (STAGE 1 IS EXTENSION STAGE)
* STATE 1 = WAREHOUSE FULL FOR WHICH:
     * ACTION 0 = STORE
     * ACTION 1 = BUY
     * ACTION 2 = SELL AND BUY
* STATE 2 = WAREHOUSE EMPTY FOR WHICH:
     * ACTION -1 = SELL
     * ACTION  0 = LEAVE EMPTY
* ACTIONS PRECEDE CURRENT STATE IN TIME
* VALUE = PROFIT SO FAR
DATA
1980 1    0     0   0
1981 0   -1    11   1
1981 1    0    -2   1
1981 1    2     1   1
1982 0    0    -1   0
1982 0   -1    13   1
1982 1    0    -2   1
1982 1    1   -12   0
1982 1    2     1   1
1983 0    0    -1   0
1983 0   -1    16   1
1983 1    0    -2   1
1983 1    1   -19   0
1983 1    2    -3   1
1984 0    0    -1   0
1984 0   -1    16   1
1984 1    0    -2   1
1984 1    1   -15   0
1984 1    2     1   1
1985 0    0    -1   0
1985 0   -1    12   1
1985 1    0    -2   1
1985 1    1   -12   0
1985 1    2     0   1
1         0    0    10   1
1         0    0     0   0
END
```

Dynacode

Dynacode can be used for forward recurrence calculations. There is no structural difference between backward and forward recurrence, it is simply a question of how the data and results are interpreted. The Dynacode input is determined by working from left to right through the decision network rather than right to left. States which were initial in the backward recurrence formulation must now be regarded as terminal, and the extension stage device is used to provide a unique

Table 2.8(b)   Warehouse problem Dynacode output for forward recurrence

```
DYNACODE WAREHOUSE PROBLEM - FORWARD RECURRENCE FORMULATION
* STAGE IS YEAR (STAGE 1 IS EXTENSION STAGE)
* STATE 1 = WAREHOUSE FULL FOR WHICH:
    * ACTION 0 = STORE
    * ACTION 1 = BUY
    * ACTION 2 = SELL AND BUY
* STATE 2 = WAREHOUSE EMPTY FOR WHICH:
    * ACTION -1 = SELL
    * ACTION  0 = LEAVE EMPTY
* ACTIONS PRECEDE CURRENT STATE IN TIME
* VALUE = PROFIT SO FAR
*
BEST ACTION LIST TO RANK      1
*
              STAGE          STATE         ACTION          VALUE
              1981             0             -1           11.000
              1981             1              2            1.000
              1982             0             -1           14.000
              1982             1              2            2.000
              1983             0             -1           18.000
              1983             1              0            0.000
              1984             0              0           17.000
              1984             1              1            3.000
              1985             0              0           16.000
              1985             1              1            5.000
                 1             0              0           16.000
*
OPTIMAL PROCESS FROM INITIAL STATE      0
*
              STAGE          STATE         ACTION          VALUE
                 1             0              0           16.000
              1985             0              0           16.000
              1984             0              0           17.000
              1983             0             -1           18.000
              1982             1              2            2.000
              1981             1              2            1.000
              1980             1              0            0.000
END
```

initial state. The forward recurrence input and output for the warehouse problem are shown in Tables 2.8(a) and 2.8(b). Rank 1 has been specified so as to provide a check on the state values in Figure 2.8.

CHAPTER 3

Discounting and a Plant Capacity Problem

3.1 Present Value

In management decision problems it is frequently necessary to use discounted cash flow methods to allow for the fact that returns arise over an extended period of time. In this chapter we show how to incorporate discounting into the decision network method. We start by introducing the ideas of discounted cash flow in relation to individual returns and sequences of returns. We then illustrate the calculations involved in decision networks with discounted returns, and finally apply the technique to a plant capacity planning problem.

Interest Rate and Discount Factor

Suppose that $100 invested for one year yields interest of $12. The interest rate is 12% per annum. $100 available now becomes $112 in one year's time.

If the full $112 is invested for another year at 12% it becomes

$$\$112(1 + 12/100) = \$125.44 \tag{3.1}$$

Investing this amount for a further year would again multiply its value by $(1 + 12/100)$, and so on for subsequent years.

If the initial amount is r and the interest rate is $x\%$, then the value after n years is

$$r(1 + x/100)^n \tag{3.2}$$

From this we see that, if money can earn interest, a given sum available now is worth more than the same amount received one or more year's later. In particular, we see that at 12% interest, $112 received in one year's time is in some sense equivalent to $100 received now. We say that $112 received in one year's time has *present value* $100. Similarly, $125.44 received in two year's time has present value $100, 12% interest.

What is the present value of $100 received in one year's time if the interest rate is 12%? This is given by

$$\$100/(1 + 12/100) = \$89.29$$

34

If the \$100 were received in two year's time its present value would be

$$\$100/(1 + 12/100)^2 = \$79.72$$

If \$r is received in n year's time and the interest rate is $x\%$ then its present value is

$$r/(1 + x/100)^n \tag{3.3}$$

Note that the present value depends on both the interest rate, x, and on the number of year's, n, from the reference date.

The expression $1/(1 + x/100)$ is called the *discount factor*. If we denote it by the symbol b then expression (3.3) becomes $b^n r$. The correspondence between interest rate and discount factor for a range of interest rates is shown in Table 3.1. Discount factors always lie in the range 0 to 1, with $b = 1$ corresponding to zero interest rate.

Table 3.1   Interest rate and discount factor

Interest rate (%)	Discount factor	Interest rate (%)	Discount factor	Interest rate (%)	Discount factor
x	$1/(1 + x/100)$	10·50	0·905	20	0·833
0·0	1·000	11·00	0·901	21	0·826
1·0	0·990	11·11	0·900	22	0·820
2·0	0·980	11·50	0·897	23	0·813
2·5	0·976	12·00	0·893	24	0·806
3·0	0·971	12·50	0·889	25	0·800
3·5	0·966	13·00	0·885	26	0·794
4·0	0·962	13·50	0·881	27	0·787
4·5	0·957	14·00	0·877	28	0·781
5·0	0·952	14·50	0·873	29	0·775
5·5	0·948	15·00	0·870	30	0·769
6·0	0·943	15·50	0·866	31	0·763
6·5	0·939	16·00	0·862	32	0·758
7·0	0·935	16·50	0·858	33	0·752
7·5	0·930	17·00	0·855	$33\frac{1}{3}$	0·750
8·0	0·926	17·50	0·851	40	0·714
8·5	0·922	18·00	0·847	50	0·667
9·0	0·917	18·50	0·844	100	0·500
9·5	0·913	19·00	0·840	150	0·400
10·0	0·909	19·50	0·837	200	0·333

Sequences of Returns

Suppose that we invest \$100 now, and as a result we receive \$70 in one year's time and \$80 in two year's time. The *net present value* of the investment is the sum of the present values of the individual amounts. Let the interest rate be 20% (this is equivalent to assuming that there is an alternate source willing to pay 20% interest on our original \$100). From Table 3.1 we see that the discount factor is 0·833. The net present value is given by

$$-100 + 0·833 \times 70 + (0·833)^2 \times 80 \tag{3.4}$$

To reduce the number of multiplications required we can write expression (3.4) as

$$-100 + 0 \cdot 833 \, (70 + 0 \cdot 833 \times 80) =$$
$$-100 + 0 \cdot 833 \, (70 + 66 \cdot 66) = 13 \cdot 88 \qquad (3.5)$$

The net present value of the investment at 20% interest rate is $13·88.

For a general sequence of returns r_0 received now, r_1 received in one year's time, up to r_n received in n year's time, the net present value at discount factor b is given by expression (3.6):

$$r_0 + br_1 + b^2 r_3 + \ldots + b^n r_n \qquad (3.6)$$

Recursive Method for Present Value Calculations

Consider, for example, a return r_0 received now and returns r_1, r_2, r_3 received in 1, 2, 3 year's time respectively. The present value given in the form of expressions (3.4) and (3.6) is as follows, where b is the discount factor:

$$r_0 + br_1 + b^2 r_2 + b^3 r_3 \qquad (3.7)$$

The most efficient way to calculate the present value is in the way used in equation (3.5). This is called the *recursive method* for present value calculations. The sequence of calculation is as indicated in expression (3.8):

$$r_0 + b[r_1 + b(r_2 + br_3)] \qquad (3.8)$$

This method is exploited in decision network calculations.

3.2 A Choice Between Two Actions

If we have to select between two alternative sequences of returns a guide to the best choice can be obtained by calculating the net present value of each sequence. The advantage will lie with the sequence which has the larger net present value. Another useful concept in assessing investment decisions is the *internal rate of return*. This is discussed at the end of this section.

In this section we give an example of choosing between two simple alternative investments. We illustrate the choice and carry out the calculation in the style of the decision network method, as a preliminary to the use of this technique in more advanced cases.

An Investment Decision

Consider a situation involving a choice between two actions 1 and 2. Under action 1 we pay $100 now and receive $132 in one year's time. Under action 2 we pay $90 now and receive $120 in one year's time. The prevailing interest rate is 25%. We wish to determine which action has the greater net present value. We can represent this choice in an elementary decision network as shown in Figure 3.1.

Action 1 has a return of -100 representing the immediate outlay of $100 the action arrow leads to an adjacent state with value 132 which represents the $132

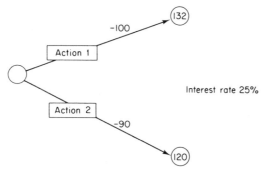

Figure 3.1   A choice between two actions

received in one year's time. Similarly for action 2 the return is −90 and the value of the adjacent state is 120. The interest rate is 25% and from Table 3.1 we see that the discount factor is 0·8.

In the decision network method we start by reducing the values of the adjacent states to present values related to the time of the current decision. We do this by multiplying the value of each state by the discount factor and entering the result on the network in brackets above the corresponding state. We have

$$0.8 \times 132 = 105.6$$
$$0.8 \times 120 = 96.0$$

The decision network is then as shown in Figure 3.2.

The decision is evaluated by computing the present value of each action and choosing the largest. For each action the present value is simply the sum of the

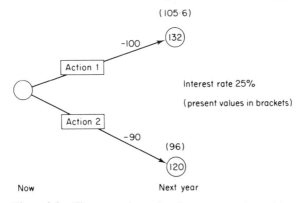

Figure 3.2   The two actions: showing present values of the adjacent states

associated return and the present value of the adjacent state, which appears in brackets above that state. Thus we have:

$$\text{Action 1:} \quad -100 + 105.6 = 5.6$$
$$\text{Action 2:} \quad -90 + 96.0 = 6.0$$

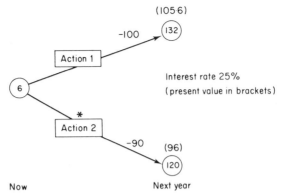

Figure 3.3   Action 2 is optimal and has net present
value $6

Hence action 2 is optimal. Its present value is $6. Figure 3.3 shows the completed network.

Note that at zero interest rate action 1 would be optimal since its undiscounted total return is $32, compared with $30 for action 2. Discounting can influence the

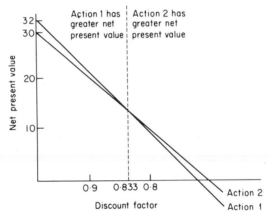

Figure 3.4   Net present value related to discount factor

choice of action as well as affecting the values involved. Figure 3.4 shows how the values of the actions vary with the discount factor.

Internal Rate of Return

For any given sequence of returns, the internal rate of return (also called the d.c.f. rate of return) is the interest rate which makes the net present value of the sequence zero. From Figure 3.4 we see that for the net present value of action 1 to be zero the discount factor must be 0·758, corresponding to an internal rate of return of 32%.

For the net present value of action 2 to be zero the discount factor must be 0·750 corresponding to an internal rate of return of 33⅓%.

The internal rate of return of an investment can be a useful indication of its quality, particularly in situations of risk, but it does have some limitations. If the returns are all positive there is no value of the internal rate of return. Some combinations of negative and positive returns can lead to multiple values of the internal rate of return. Also, it gives no indication of the magnitude of the yield involved at a realistic interest rate. For these reasons net present value is a more satisfactory investment criterion, although internal rate of return is also a useful concept.

In many practical situations any of a large number of sequences of returns may result, depending on a sequence of decisions which is made over an extended time period. It is here that the decision network method is valuable. It provides a conceptual and visual framework for the decision process. At the same time it provides a method for evaluating and optimizing net present value. For interrelated decisions in systems which have the Markov property the calculation method is much more efficient than the separate evaluation of each individual return sequence.

3.3 Plant Capacity Planning

A company has a plant which, at the beginning of 1981, has a production capacity of 10 units on some suitable scale. The company is planning over the three-year period to the beginning of 1984 and it has decided that throughout this time the capacity must be not less than 10 units and not more than 12 units. Within these constraints, in any year the capacity level may be increased or decreased by one unit, or may remain unchanged. The return generated by the plant in any year depends on the capacity at the start of the year, any change in capacity which occurs within the year, and on the market situation in the year. Assessments of the market prospects and of the costs of capacity changes have been made for the planning period. The value of the plant at the end of the period has also been assessed, with different values attributable, depending on the final capacity level.

Table 3.2 Profit and cost assessments

Year	Capacity level	Profit from sales	Cost if capacity increased	Saving if capacity decreased	Relative plant value
1981	10	2	5		
1982	10	3	7		
1982	11	7	3	1	
1983	10	4	9		
1983	11	9	8	1	
1983	12	12		2	
1984	10				0
1984	11				2
1984	12				4

40

The results of these profit and cost assessments are shown in Table 3.2. The relative plant value is value of the plant in 1984 at the stated capacity, minus its value at a capacity of 10 units.

The company wishes to decide what the production capacity should be in each year in order to maximize the net present value of total returns (including relative plant value) over the planning period, with discounting at an interest rate of 10% per year.

Formulation

To derive a decision network for the problem we start by considering the situation in 1981. The decision at the beginning of 1981 is illustrated in Figure 3.5.

In Figure 3.5 the initial production capacity is 10 units. In 1981 we can either leave the production capacity unchanged or increase it by one unit. A decrease is

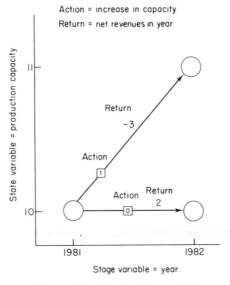

Figure 3.5   The decision in 1981

not allowed because a minimum capacity of 10 units has been specified. The state variable is the production capacity at the start of a year. The stage variable is the year number. The action variable is the change in capacity within the year. The return associated with an action is given by the profit from sales minus or plus the cost or saving from capacity changes, in the year. Thus, if there is no change in capacity in 1981 the return is 2 units, corresponding to the profit from sales indicated in the first row of Table 3.2. If capacity is increased so that it reaches 11 units by the start of 1982 the return is −3, given by the profit from sales of 2 units minus the cost of increasing capacity which is 5 units as shown in the first row of Table 3.2. For each action the adjacent state is the capacity level at the start of the following year.

Extending the principles of Figure 3.5 we obtain a decision network for the whole problem which is shown in Figure 3.6.

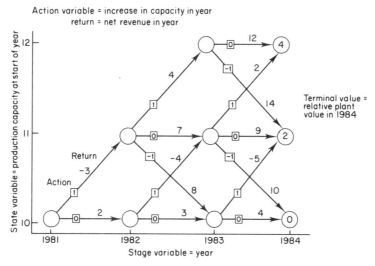

Figure 3.6   Plant capacity planning: the decision network

When profits and costs arise in the course of a year and discounting is to be applied, then for precise accuracy all amounts should be discounted back to the start of the year.

Calculations

The calculations follow a similar sequence to the undiscounted case, but discounting of the returns is introduced in one of two ways. These are as follows.

1. Pre-discounted Method. Discount the terminal values and all the returns back to present values with respect to the initial date (or any reference date). Replace the undiscounted data by this discounted data and then solve the problem in the standard way. In this method the state values will all be expressed as present values with respect to the initial (or reference) date.

2. Recursive Discounting. The terminal values and returns appear on the network in undiscounted form. At each stage the values of the adjacent states are multiplied by the discount factor, reducing them to present values with respect to the current stage.

Recursive discounting is the usual method for decision network calculations. It has the advantage that the data appear in undiscounted form and do not vary with changes in the interest rate or the time origin. The method is similar in principle to the recursive method for present value calculations described in Section 3.1, expression (3.8). The state values appear as present values with respect to their own point in time. The optimal and other policies found are the same by either method.

The calculations, which employ the usual backward and forward pass technique are now described in detail for the plant capacity problem. The recursive method of discounting will be used. The calculation starts with the determination of the discount factor. The interest rate is 10% so the discount factor is 0·909 from Table 3.1. The procedure at each stage is then as follows:

(1) Multiply the values of the adjacent states by the discount factor and place the result in brackets above each state.

(2) Carry out the usual optimization calculations using the discounted values of the adjacent states.

The Decisions in 1983

We start by discounting the values of the terminal states and writing the discounted values in brackets above the corresponding states in the network. For stage 1984, the values of states 10, 11, 12 respectively are 0, 2, 4 and so the discounted values are given by:

$$0·909 \times 0 = 0$$
$$0·909 \times 2 = 1·818$$
$$0·909 \times 4 = 3·636$$

These values are written above the states in Figure 3.8. They are the present values of the terminal states with respect to 1983.

We then carry out the optimization calculations for 1983. We shall consider state 10 first, that is a production capacity of 10 units. The actions are evaluated by adding the returns at the current stage to the present values of the adjacent states.

The decision at state 10, stage 1983, is shown in Figure 3.7. There are two actions available, namely to retain the existing capacity (action 0) or to increase capacity (action 1). Under action 0 the return is 4 units, the adjacent state is state 10, and its present value is 0. Under action 1 the return is −5 units, the adjacent state is state 11 which has present value 1·818. The values of the actions are as follows:

$$\text{Action 0:} \quad 4 + 0 \quad = 4$$
$$\text{Action 1:} \quad -5 + 1·818 = -3·182$$

Action 0 gives the larger net present value of future returns and is optimal for this state. The optimal value of 4 units is written in the node. Optimal actions are indicated by an asterisk near the node label.

State 11 at stage 1983 is considered next. The actions are evaluated as follows:

$$\text{Action} -1: \quad 10 + 0 \quad = 10$$
$$\text{Action} \quad 0: \quad 9 + 1·818 = 10·818$$
$$\text{Action} \quad 1: \quad 2 + 3·636 = 5·636$$

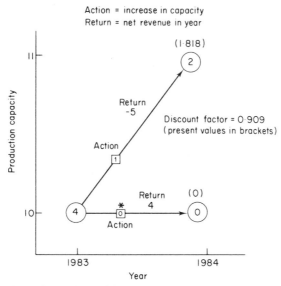

Figure 3.7   The decision at production capacity level 10
in 1983

Action 0 gives the largest net present value of future returns and is optimal. The value 10·818 is written in the node. This is the net present value of future returns from this state, calculated with respect to the date of the state, that is 1983. This result is shown in Figure 3.8.

Continuing to state 12 at stage 1983 we find that action −1 is optimal and that the present value is 15·818. The optimization for 1983 is now concluded.

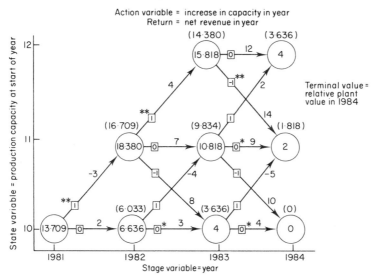

Figure 3.8   Plant capacity planning: the completed decision network

The Decisions in 1982

The next stage starts with discounting the values of the 1983 states, converting them into present values with respect to 1982. For states 10, 11, and 12 respectively we multiply the optimal values (shown in the nodes, Figure 3.8) by the discount factor and get the values shown in the brackets above the nodes, thus

$$0\cdot909 \times 4 \qquad = 3\cdot636$$
$$0\cdot909 \times 10\cdot818 = 9\cdot834$$
$$0\cdot909 \times 15\cdot818 = 14\cdot380$$

The calculations have been carried out to more than three decimal place accuracy and then rounded to three decimal places.

The optimization for 1982 then follows. For state 10 the actions are evaluated:

$$\text{Action 0:} \qquad 3 + 3\cdot636 = 6\cdot636$$
$$\text{Action 1:} \qquad -4 + 9\cdot834 = 5\cdot834$$

Action 0 is optimal. The value 6·636 is written in the node. This is the maximum present value of the total future return generated from state 10 and stage 1982, discounted with respect to 1982.

At state 11 we find that action 1 is optimal and has value 18·380. Optimization at stage 1982 is then concluded.

The Decision in 1981

We next discount the values of states 10 and 11 at stage 1982 and get

$$0\cdot909 \times 6\cdot636 = 6\cdot033$$
$$0\cdot909 \times 18\cdot380 = 16\cdot709$$

Optimization at stage 1981, state 10 yields:

$$\text{Action 0:} \qquad 2 + 6\cdot033 = 8\cdot033$$
$$\text{Action 1:} \qquad -3 + 16\cdot709 = 13\cdot709$$

Hence action 1 is optimal and the maximum present value of future returns, discounted with respect to 1981, is 13·707 units. The backward pass is now concluded.

The Forward Pass

The forward pass is the same as for undiscounted problems. We start at the initial state, in this case state 10 at stage 1981, and pick out the path indicated by asterisks, marking it with a second asterisk against each action used. The double asterisks then indicate the optimal path. The optimal plan is shown in Table 3.3. The cash flows in the various years are shown undiscounted and discounted to 1981 in Table 3.4.

Table 3.3   Plant capacity: the optimal plan

Stage (year)	State (production capacity)	Action (change in capacity)	Value (present value of maximum future returns)
1981	10	1	13·709
1982	11	1	18·380
1983	12	−1	15·818
1984	11		2·000

Table 3.4   Plant capacity: cash flows (undiscounted)

Stage (year)	State (production capacity)	Action (change in capacity)	Return (cash flow)	
			undiscounted	discounted
1981	10	1	−3	−3
1982	11	1	4	3·636
1983	12	−1	14	11·568

3.4 Computer Method

The Dynacode input for the plant capacity problem is shown in Table 3.5. The principles followed are the same as in the shortest-path problem, Section 1.6 of Chapter 1. This problem involves maximization. There are 3 terminal states. The requirement for discounting is indicated by the presence of the PERCENT x, where x is a positive real number, in this case 10. This indicates that returns are to be discounted at 10% per stage. The data follow exactly the same pattern as for the shortest-path problem, and are given in undiscounted form. The calculation of the discount factor and its application using the recursive method are carried out internally by Dynacode. Thus the only difference in the input between an undiscounted and a discounted problem is in the inclusion of the statement PERCENT x in the program. To change the interest rate we change the value of x and rerun the problem. For example, in the present case, to change to $12\frac{1}{2}$% interest we would replace the statement PERCENT 10 by the statement PERCENT 12·5.

The Dynacode output is shown in Table 3.6. This confirms the results obtained in the hand calculations (Table 3.3).

3.5 Algebraic Summary

Let x be the interest rate per cent. The discount factor b is given by $b = 1/(1 + x/100)$. Following the definitions and terminology of Section 2.6 we let n be the stage variable, i the state variable, k the action variable, and $r(n, i, k)$ be

Table 3.5   Dynacode input for the plant capacity problem

DYNACODE PLANT CAPACITY PROBLEM—DECISION NETWORKS
LIST INPUT
TERMINAL STATES 3
PERCENT 10
* STAGE IS YEAR
* STATE IS CAPACITY AT START OF YEAR
* ACTION IS CHANGE IN CAPACITY
* VALUE IS PRESENT VALUE OF TOTAL FUTURE RETURN
DATA

Stage	State	Action	Terminal value or return	Adjacent state	
1984	10	0	0	0	Terminal states
1984	11	0	2	0	
1984	12	0	4	0	
1983	10	0	4	10	
1983	10	1	−5	11	
1983	11	−1	10	10	
1983	11	0	9	11	
1983	11	1	2	12	
1983	12	−1	14	11	
1983	12	0	12	12	
1982	10	0	3	10	
1982	10	1	−4	11	
1982	11	−1	8	10	
1982	11	0	7	11	
1982	11	1	4	12	
1981	10	0	2	10	
1981	10	1	−3	11	
END					

Table 3.6   Dynacode output for plant capacity problem

DYNACODE PLANT CAPACITY PROBLEM—DECISION NETWORKS
* STAGE IS YEAR
* STATE IS CAPACITY AT START OF YEAR
* ACTION IS CHANGE IN CAPACITY
* VALUE IS PRESENT VALUE OF TOTAL FUTURE RETURN
*
OPTIMAL PROCESS FROM INITIAL STATE 10
*
INTEREST RATE PERCENT
         10.000
*

STAGE	STATE	ACTION	VALUE
1981	10	1	13.709
1982	11	1	18.380
1983	12	−1	15.818
1984	11	0	2.000

the return associated with stage n, state i and action k. $r(n, i, k)$ is the undiscounted return, except that where it consists of components generated over the course of a stage then these should be discounted back to the start of the stage.

Recursive discounting involves multiplying the values of the adjacent states by the discount factor at each stage. The dynamic programming recurrence relation is then as follows:

$$f(n, i) = \underset{k}{\text{Max}} \, [r(n, i, k) + bf(n + 1, j)] \qquad (3.9)$$

Here $f(n, i)$ is the present value of future returns related to stage n as origin.

If the stages are numbered $n = 0, 1, 2, 3 \ldots$ with the origin at the present point in time then the pre-discounted method is summarized by

$$f(n, i) = \underset{k}{\text{Max}} \, [b^n r(n, i, k) + f(n + 1, j)] \qquad (3.10)$$

Here $f(n, i)$ is the present value of future returns related to stage 0 as origin.

CHAPTER 4

Workforce, Vehicle Fleet Capacity, and Replacement Problems

4.1 Capacity Problems

In this chapter we illustrate the application of the decision network method to some problems of capacity planning and to a replacement problem. In capacity planning the general situation is that one has certain capacity requirements which vary with time over a planning period. The requirements can be met by increasing or decreasing workforce, vehicle fleet, etc. However, it may be impractical or undesirable to vary, for example, the workforce level strictly in step with requirements and this will mean the use of overtime or the carrying of excess labour. In the case of vehicles, shortages can be made up by buying, and in other cases subcontracting or the diversion of work to less suitable plant may be necessary. The decision network method can be used as a planning framework for these problems and can indicate policies which achieve minimum cost, or which reflect other utilities such as minimizing overtime and/or short time working. We consider firstly a workforce planning problem and secondly a vehicle fleet capacity problem. The chapter concludes with a machine replacement problem.

4.2 A Workforce Planning Problem

Work Schedule

A construction company has a work schedule on a certain site which requires the following numbers of full time steel erectors in the months indicated:

Month	March	April	May	June	July	August
Men	4	6	7	4	6	2

There are to be three steel erectors on the site in September.

Transfer Costs

Men work at the site on a monthly basis and in February there were three steel

48

erectors on the site. The cost of transferring in additional men is $50 per man and the cost of transferring men out to another site is $80 per man.

Transfer Rules

It is not feasible to transfer in more than three men in any month and under a union agreement not more than one third of the current manpower in any trade can be transferred out from a site at the end of a month, except on completion of a contract.

Short Time and Overtime

The cost of having surplus steel erectors is $100 per man per month and the cost of having a shortage (which must be made up in overtime) is $200 per man (equivalent full time) per month. Overtime cannot exceed 25% of normal time.

Problems

It is feasible to meet the work schedule with the constraints given? How many men should be transferred into or from the site each month in order to: (a) minimize total costs; and (b) minimize the total man-days of short time and overtime working.

4.3 Formulation and Minimum Cost Solution

We first consider drawing a network to determine whether it is feasible to meet the work schedule within the constraints and at the same time we calculate the costs required to determine a minimum cost solution.

Timing of Transfers

In our formulation of the problem we shall assume that all transfers occur at the end of a month, incurring a cost in the month in which they occur. For example, if there were four men on site in December and two were transferred out at the end of that month, a transfer cost of $160 would be incurred in December and two men would be on site in January. Then if one man was transferred in at the end of January a transfer cost of $50 would be incurred in January and three men would be on site in February. Equally, one could assume that transfers occur and costs arise at the beginning of a month. Either assumption will lead to a valid formulation provided that it is used consistently. The advantage of assuming that transfers occur at the end of a month is that the state variable is then the number of men actually on site during a month, and hence the decision network has a straightforward interpretation as a plot of workforce level against time.

February Transfers

In February there are three men on site and in March four are needed. Overtime cannot exceed 25% so that three men cannot do the work of four. Hence the March requirement cannot be met unless we transfer in at least one man at the end of February.

If the number of men we could transfer in in any month were restricted we would need to consider recruitment in anticipation of future need. This does not apply in the problem as stated so we need not consider recruitment beyond the requirements of the following month. From this we conclude that the only feasible action at the end of February is to transfer in one man.

We can represent this action and the associated cost of $50 as shown in Figure 4.1. There the lower left-hand node represents there being three men on site during

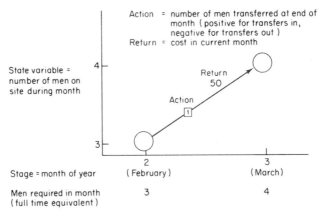

Figure 4.1   At the end of February one man is transferred in
at a cost of $50

February. The upper right-hand node represents there being four men on site during March. The action variable, which has the value 1 represents the transfer in of one man at the end of February at a cost of $50. Note that the transfer action and the corresponding cost incurred at the end of February are associated with the February stage in this formulation.

The state variable is the number of men on site during a given month. The stage variable is the month of the year. The action variable is the number of men transferred at the end of the month, positive for transfers in and negative for transfers out. The return is the cost in the current month and is made up by the transfer costs plus overtime or short time costs if any. The adjacent state is the number of men on site next month.

March Transfers

From the last subsection we know that four men will be on site in March. In April six men (equivalent full time) are needed. There are two ways in which this requirement can be met and these are:

(i) Transfer in one man at the end of March, at cost $50. The labour force will then be 5 in April. The equivalent of one additional full-time man can be made up by working 20% overtime in April.

(ii) Transfer in two men at the end of March at cost $100. The labour force will be 6 in April and the requirement then will be met without overtime.

There is no overtime or short time in March (since the four men available exactly match the requirement). The actions and costs up to the end of March are

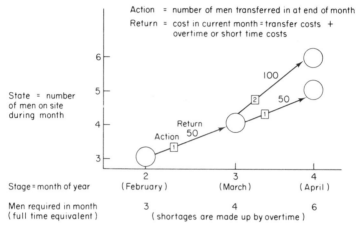

Figure 4.2   Workforce planning: feasible actions for February and March

therefore as shown in Figure 4.2. Overtime costs to be incurred in April do not appear on this network.

April Costs and Transfers

In April we may have five men or six men on site depending on the action adopted in March. Consider firstly the situation where five men are on site. The work schedule calls for six men so overtime equivalent to one man is required. This costs $200. The schedule calls for seven men in May and this can be achieved by seven men or by six men with overtime. Five men are insufficient since overtime would exceed 25%. Thus two actions are available with costs and adjacent states as shown in the following table:

Action variable = men transferred in at end of month	Costs			Adjacent state = workforce in May
	Overtime	Transfers	Total	
1	200	50	250	6
2	200	100	300	7

If we have six men on site in April no overtime cost is incurred. The actions available are to transfer no men (cost zero) or to transfer in one man at cost $50.

The Complete Network

The rest of the decision network is built up in the way described for March and April. The limitations on overtime, and on the number of transfers out, and the requirement to have only three men on site in September restrict the actions available to those shown in Figure 4.3. We see that it is feasible to meet the manpower requirements of the site. This figure also shows the complete decision network calculations for a minimum cost solution, and the transfers required by this solution.

4.4 Minimizing Overtime and Short Time Working

The use of decision networks is not confined to cost minimization or profit maximization applications. Any objective which can be expressed as the mathematical equivalent of maximizing or minimizing the total return generated, with or without discounting, is suitable. Certain other objectives can also be handled, such as multiplicative and 'max–min' returns. These rarely arise in management decision problems and are not considered in this book. They are discussed in books on dynamic programming, e.g., Hastings (1973, Chap. 1).

From Figure 4.3 we can see all the transfer actions which are available under the rules governing overtime and workforce reduction. If we wanted to arrange the transfers so that short time working is minimized it is obvious that we can do this by keeping the labour force as small as possible. From Figure 4.3 the transfers for this would be February 1, March 1, April 1, May −2, June 1, July −1, August −1.

Overtime can be minimized by keeping the labour force large. At an extreme, the labour force could be at the maximum level throughout. This is, in fact, the same as the minimum cost solution in this case. The point is that the overtime and short time implications of various transfer policies can be seen directly from the network, even without any further adjustments or formal calculations.

Utility

By changing the returns on the network we can evaluate policies which reflect various utilities. By utility, in this sense, we mean a measure of usefulness other than money. For example, management experience suggests that it is advisable to have a pattern of regular working on the construction site, with both overtime and short time working kept to a minimum. We can find a plan which minimizes short time and overtime working by changing the returns in the decision network from costs to man-months of short time or overtime. This is illustrated in Figure 4.4. The minimum number of man-days of short time plus overtime is 3 and there are two solutions which achieve this. These are shown in Figure 4.4.

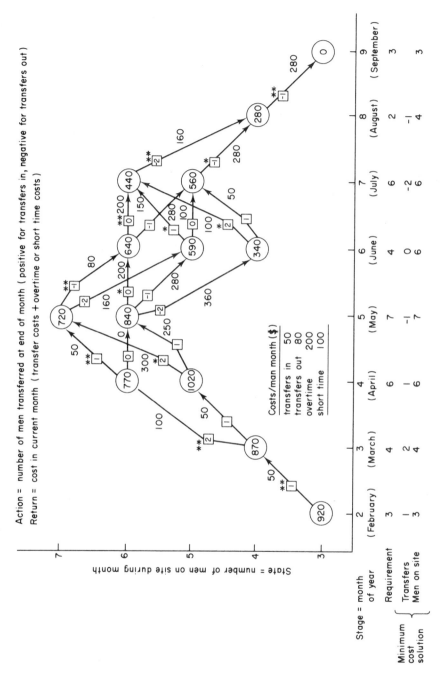

Figure 4.3 Workforce planning problem: the decision network with minimum cost solution

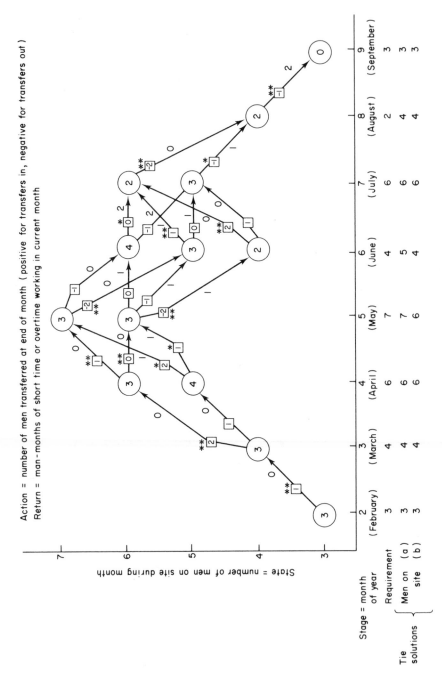

Figure 4.4 Workforce planning problem: decision network with solutions for minimum overtime plus short time working

The utilities employed in this example are mathematically equivalent to a cost structure in which the cost per man-month of overtime and short time are each one unit and the cost of transfers is zero. Yet another utility structure could be used to minimize the number of months in which either short time or overtime is worked, without regard to number of men short or in surplus. Finally, it should be said that ordinary costs represent some form of overall utility placed on a good by a particular society and that departures from realistic costing practices should not be adopted lightly.

Other Constraints and Factors

Other constraints and factors can be incorporated into workforce planning networks. The following are some examples:

(a) Limited recruitment. The number of men transferred in (or recruited) in any period may be limited. The action variable which represents net increase in manpower in a time period is then confined to the specified maximum. The constraint may vary through time, reflecting changes in the labour market.

(b) Limited proportion of recruits. The number of men recruited in any period may be limited to a certain proportion of those already employed because it may be impractical or undesirable to have more than a certain proportion of trainees.

(c) Resignation wastage. Wastage can be allowed for in several ways. For example: (i) Any known pattern of wastage dependent on time only can be imposed. (ii) A proportion of the current labour force can be assumed to resign at the end of each month. The proportion may be time dependent. (iii) When the actual labour position is known at the start of a month the corresponding state is the starting point of the required optimal path.

(d) Stochastic models. A stochastic process is a sequence of random variables. A stochastic model is a model in which probabilistic events are considered, e.g. in the workforce planning model, probabilities may be associated with various levels of recruitment and wastage in different time periods. Stochastic models are considered later in the book.

4.5 Computer Method

The Dynacode input is shown in Table 4.1. The principles followed are the same as for the shortest-path problem (Section 1.6, Chapter 1). Note that the Dynacode data can be written down directly from the decision network. To do this we start with the terminal state and then work over the network in the same sequence as is used in the backward pass of calculation. There is one line of data for each arrow in the network. The Dynacode output is shown in Table 4.2.

DYNACODE WORKFORCE PLANNING—DECISION NETWORKS
LIST INPUT
MINIMIZE
TERMINAL STATES 1
* STAGE IS MONTH OF YEAR
* STATE IS NUMBER OF MEN ON SITE
* ACTION IS NUMBER TRANSFERRED (POSITIVE FOR TRANSFERS
*   IN, NEGATIVE FOR TRANSFERS OUT)
DATA

Stage	State	Action	Terminal value or return	Adjacent state
9	3	0	0	0
8	4	−1	280	3
7	5	−1	280	4
7	6	−2	160	4
6	4	1	50	5
6	4	2	100	6
6	5	0	100	5
6	5	1	150	6
6	6	−1	280	5
6	6	0	200	6
5	6	−2	360	4
5	6	−1	280	5
5	6	0	200	6
5	7	−2	160	5
5	7	−1	80	6
4	5	1	250	6
4	5	2	300	7
4	6	0	0	6
4	6	1	50	7
3	4	1	50	5
3	4	2	100	6
2	3	1	50	4

END

Table 4.2   Workforce planning problem: Dynacode output

DYNACODE WORKFORCE PLANNING—DECISION NETWORKS
* STAGE IS MONTH OF YEAR
* STATE IS NUMBER OF MEN ON SITE
* ACTION IS NUMBER OF TRANSFERRED (POSITIVE FOR TRANSFERS
*   IN, NEGATIVE FOR TRANSFERS OUT)
*

OPTIMAL PROCESS
*

STAGE	STATE	ACTION	VALUE
2	3	1	920.000
3	4	2	870.000
4	6	1	770.000
5	7	−1	720.000
6	6	0	640.000
7	6	−2	440.000
8	4	−1	280.000
9	3	0	0.000

Problem

A company is planning the capacity of its vehicle fleet in the period 1987 to 1991. The company has some hundreds of vehicles which it divides into groups by types, e.g. cars, light vans, medium vans, trucks, etc. We shall develop a decision network relating to trucks, similar networks could be developed for other groups.

In the first year of the planning period, that is 1987, the company has 10 trucks. Sales of old trucks and purchases of new ones take place only at the end of a year. Trucks are sold when they reach 7 years of age. From an analysis of the age of vehicles in the current fleet the number of trucks to be sold in each year of the planning period can be determined. Capacity requirements over the planning period have been assessed and the following table shows the capacity requirement in each year and also the number of trucks to be sold in that year:

Year	1987	1988	1989	1990	1991
Capacity requirement	10	11	9	12	12
Vehicles to be sold	1	0	2	1	

For planning purposes it is to be assumed that the company will have 12 trucks in 1991. New trucks cost $12,000 each and old ones are sold for $1000 each. Shortages of capacity can be made up by hiring at $2000 per truck per year. It is company policy to meet at least base load requirements with its own fleet and for present planning purposes we are to assume that the number of trucks owned by the company must never be less than 9. To avoid disproportionate cash flow effects in individual years the number of trucks purchased in any year must not exceed 3. Determine a hiring and purchasing plan which minimizes the present value of total costs with discounting at an interest rate of 15% per year.

Formulation

In 1987 we have 10 trucks and at the end of that year 1 must be sold, leaving 9. In 1988 we need 11 trucks so we must acquire 2 by hiring or purchase. That is, the purchase quantity at the end of 1987 may be 0, 1 or 2. This decision is shown in Figure 4.5.

As in the case of transfers of men in the workforce planning model, we shall assume that purchases and sales occurring at the turn of a year relate to the year which is ending. Thus purchases and sales at the end of 1987/beginning of 1988, relate to 1987. The cost of sales and purchases incurred at this time are therefore related to 1987 and for consistency must be discounted back to the start of that year. This type of assumption allows us to develop a network in which the state variable is the size of the vehicle fleet in the current year. One could develop a logically consistent model in which the cost of purchases at the turn of the year 1987/8 was related to 1988 but in this case the state variable for 1988 would be the size of the vehicle fleet in 1987. This makes it less easy to interpret the fleet size from the network.

58

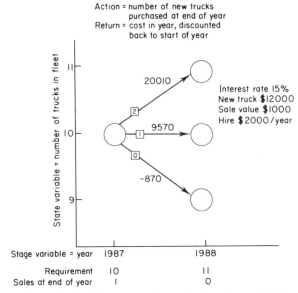

Figure 4.5   Vehicle fleet problem: the decision in 1987

In a discounted network the return associated with an action is assumed to arise at the beginning of the year in which the action takes place, or if it does not, to be expressed as a present value with respect to the beginning of the year. In many cases the fact that returns accumulate during a year rather than arising exactly at the beginning would be a negligible factor. In the present case, however, major expenditure occurs at the end of the year and there would be significant loss of accuracy if this cost were not discounted back to the beginning of the year. For example, a truck is bought for $12,000 at the end of 1987; the cost of this is attributed to the year 1987 and needs to be expressed as a present value at the start of 1987. The interest rate is 15%. From Table 3.1 the discount factor is 0·87. Hence the present value of $12,000 at the beginning of the year is 0·87 × 12,000 = $10,440. Similar considerations apply to income from sales of trucks, which arises at the end of a year. Hire charges, on the other hand are assumed to be payable at the beginning of the year to which they relate. To calculate the returns associated with various actions it is convenient to make a table showing costs related to the start of the year when various numbers of trucks are bought, sold and hired. This is as follows:

Number of trucks	Buy $12,000 per truck	Sell $1000 per truck	Hire $2000 per truck
	Cost discounted to start of year		
1	10,440	−870	2000
2	20,880	−1740	4000
3	31,320		

Returning to the decision for 1987, we are now able to calculate the returns. No trucks are hired since the fleet capacity meets requirements. One truck is sold at the end of the year for $1000. In terms of present values at the start of the year, this realizes $870. If no trucks are purchased the return is −870 (see Figure 4.5). If one truck is bought the present value of the purchase price is $10,440. Hence the return is $10,440 − $870 = $9570. If two trucks are purchased the return is $20,880 −$870 = $20,010. Figure 4.5 illustrates this.

The formulation can be summarized as follows. The stage variable is the year number. The state variable is the number of trucks in the fleet. The action variable is the number of trucks purchased. Purchases and sales occur at the end of a year. The adjacent state variable is the number of trucks in the fleet next year. This is equal to the number this year plus the number purchased at the end of the year, minus the number sold at the end of the current year. The return variable is the net cost incurred this year. The return is given by the hiring costs plus the discounted purchase costs minus the discounted proceeds of sales. Note that the formulation depends on us being able to determine in advance the number of sales in each year of the planning period. This can be done provided that the planning period is longer than the life of a vehicle. Otherwise the pattern of purchases early in the period would influence later sales and this would destroy the Markov property. No attempt is made to reflect the age distribution of vehicles, as this would lead to a network with a very large number of nodes.

Calculations

The complete network and all the calculations are shown in Figure 4.6. Recursive discounting has been used for these calculations, following the method described

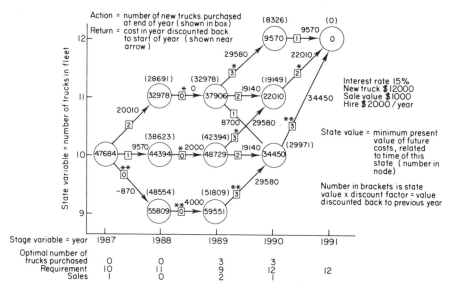

Figure 4.6   Vehicle fleet capacity: the complete decision network

in Section 3.3, Chapter 3. The value of a state (the number in the node) is the minimum present value of future costs, related to the date of that state. The optimal numbers of trucks to be purchased are: 1987, zero; 1988, zero; 1989, three; 1990, three. The present value of total future costs at the start of 1987 is $47,684.

4.7 A Machine Replacement Problem

A group of 20 identical machines is used in a production process. The machines are part of a plant which has a remaining life of 5 years. Each year every machine must be either overhauled or replaced. New machines cost $20,000 each. Table 4.3 shows the age distribution of the existing machines at the start of the 5-year

Table 4.3   Machine overhaul costs, sale values, and initial age distribution

Age in years	1	2	3	4
Number of machines	5	4	8	3
Cost of overhaul ($1000s)	7	3	9	
Sale value ($1000s)	10	5	2	0

New machines cost $20,000. All costs are per machine.

period. It also shows the cost of overhaul and the sale value of the machines, which are dependent upon age. 4-year-old machines must be replaced. There are no new machines initially since the planning period starts just before a replacement/overhaul decision point.

Determine a replacement plan which minimizes the present value of future costs at an interest rate of 25% per year. Determine also the numbers of machines to be replaced and overhauled in each year and the resulting cash requirements under the minimum cost plan.

Formulation

We shall formulate a decision network which enables us to determine the best overhaul/replacement decisions for machines of any age, at any point in the planning period. A stage in the decision process corresponds to a year. Let the stage variable be the number of years remaining in the planning period, initially this is 5. Consider the initial decision required for a particular machine. For purposes of illustration let the machine we are considering be 3 years old. It now requires to be either replaced or overhauled.

Let 'replace' be action 1 and 'overhaul' be action 2. The costs and results of these actions for the 3-year-old machine are as follows.

Action 1 (Replace). The existing machine is sold for 2 units (we shall work in units of $1000) and a new machine is purchased for 20 units. The net cost is 18 units. The new machine is, of course, initially of age 0, but by the next decision point, which is in 1 year's time, it becomes a machine of age 1.

Action 2 (Overhaul). The existing machine is overhauled at a cost of 9 units (costs are given in Table 4.3). At the next decision point in 1 year's time this machine will have reached age 4.

The initial decision for a machine of age 3 is shown in Figure 4.7. The formulation is as follows. The stage variable is the number of years remaining in the planning period, initially 5. The state variable is the age of a machine at a point where

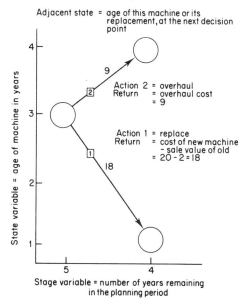

Figure 4.7   Machine replacement: the decision
for a 3-year-old machine at stage 5

a replace/overhaul decision is required. This ranges from 1 to 4. (4-year-old machines must be replaced, but nominally we regard age 4 as a decision point.) Action 1 is replace, action 2 is overhaul. The return is the cost in the current year. Under action 1 (replace) this is the cost of a new machine minus the sale value of the old one. Under action 2 (overhaul) the return is the cost of overhaul. The adjacent state is the age at the next decision point, of either this machine or the one which replaces it. Whenever a machine is replaced the age at the next decision point is 1 year, because the new machine becomes 1 year old by the time the decision point is reached. For overhaul at age i the adjacent state is the age next year which is $i + 1$. The terminal values are minus the sale values at the corresponding ages. These are negative because they represent income in a cost minimization problem. The value of a state is the minimum present value of total cost over the planning period for a machine which starts at the corresponding state and age. In this formulation decisions occur and costs arise at the beginning of a year and there is no need to consider discounting back to the start of a year the returns which arise in that year. The interest rate is 25%, corresponding to a discount factor of 0·8, from Table 3.1.

Hand Calculations

The hand calculations are shown on the decision network in Figure 4.8. This figure shows the optimal replacement/overhaul action for every age of vehicle

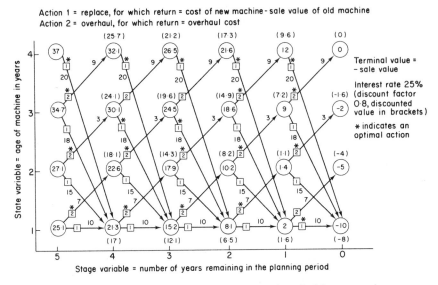

Figure 4.8 Machine replacement: the complete decision network

throughout the planning period. The state values are the minimum present values of future costs. Recursive discounting has been used, following the method described in Section 3.3, Chapter 3. The optimal sequence of actions for a particular machine depends on its age at the start of the planning period. The optimal actions are summarized in Table 4.4, which indicates the action to be taken for a machine of a given age at a given point in time.

Table 4.4 Machine replacement: optimal actions

Age	Years remaining				
	5	4	3	2	1
1	overhaul	overhaul	overhaul	overhaul	replace
2	overhaul	overhaul	overhaul	overhaul	overhaul
3	overhaul	replace	replace	overhaul	overhaul
4	replace	replace	replace	replace	replace

Computer Calculations

The Dynacode input for the machine replacement problem is shown in Table 4.5. From the decision network (Figure 4.8) we see that the states, actions, and returns

Table 4.5   Machine replacement: Dynacode input

DYNACODE MACHINE REPLACEMENT—DECISION NETWORKS
LIST INPUT
MINIMIZE
STATIONARY
STAGES 5
TERMINAL STATES 4
PERCENT 25
* STAGE IS NUMBER OF YEARS TO END OF PLANNING PERIOD
* STATE IS AGE OF MACHINE
* ACTION 1 IS REPLACE
* ACTION 2 IS OVERHAUL
* VALUE IS PRESENT VALUE OF FUTURE COSTS
   IN THOUSAND OF DOLLARS
DATA

stage	state	action	terminal value or return	adjacent state	
0	1	0	−10	0	terminal
0	2	0	−5	0	states
0	3	0	−2	0	
0	4	0	0	0	
1	1	1	10	1	
1	1	2	7	2	stage 1
1	2	1	15	1	data, which
1	2	2	3	3	is also used
1	3	1	18	1	at the other
1	3	2	9	4	stages
1	4	1	20	1	

END

---

are the same at every stage. A problem for which the data are the same at every stage is said to be stationary. If the data are the same for a few stages but then change, the problem is not stationary. We indicate that the problem is stationary by entering the statement STATIONARY in the Dynacode program. The data then consist of the terminal value entries (unless set to zero, see next paragraph) followed by the data for stage 1. The states must be in the same order in the terminal value and stage 1 data; in the current problem this order is 1, 2, 3, 4. The computer stores the stage 1 data and re-uses it at each subsequent stage. We must indicate how many stages there are and this is done by means of a statement STAGES *n* where *n* is the number of stages. In the present case there are five stages and the statement STAGES 5 appears in the program. In stationary problems the stages are automatically labelled 0, 1, 2, 3, etc., with stage 0 being the terminal stage.

In stationary problems (including infinite stage and semi-Markov problems which are discussed later), in which the user desires to set all the terminal values to zero, use can be made of the statement ZERO TERMINAL VALUES. When this statement appears in the program, Dynacode sets the values of the terminal states to zero and the user does not supply the terminal values as part of the data. The statement ZERO TERMINAL VALUES can only be used in stationary, infinite

Table 4.6   Machine replacement: Dynacode output

```
DYNACODE MACHINE REPLACEMENT - DECISION NETWORKS
* STAGE IS NUMBER OF YEARS TO END OF PLANNING PERIOD
* STATE IS AGE OF MACHINE
* ACTION 1 IS REPLACE
* ACTION 2 IS OVERHAUL
* VALUE IS PRESENT VALUE OF FUTURE COSTS
*
OPTIMAL PROCESS FROM INITIAL STATE      1
*
     INTEREST RATE PERCENT
         25.000
*
         STAGE          STATE          ACTION          VALUE
           5              1               2            25.077
           4              2               2            22.596
           3              3               1            24.496
           2              1               2             8.119
           1              2               2             1.399
           0              3               0            -2.000
*
OPTIMAL PROCESS FROM INITIAL STATE      2
*
     INTEREST RATE PERCENT
         25.000
*
         STAGE          STATE          ACTION          VALUE
           5              2               2            27.102
           4              3               1            30.128
           3              1               2            15.160
           2              2               2            10.199
           1              3               2             9.000
           0              4               0             0.000
*
OPTIMAL PROCESS FROM INITIAL STATE      3
*
     INTEREST RATE PERCENT
         25.000
*
         STAGE          STATE          ACTION          VALUE
           5              3               2            34.702
           4              4               1            32.128
           3              1               2            15.160
           2              2               2            10.199
           1              3               2             9.000
           0              4               0             0.000
*
OPTIMAL PROCESS FROM INITIAL STATE      4
*
     INTEREST RATE PERCENT
         25.000
*
         STAGE          STATE          ACTION          VALUE
           5              4               1            37.043
           4              1               2            21.304
           3              2               2            17.880
           2              3               2            18.600
           1              4               1            12.000
           0              1               0           -10.000
END
```

stage or semi-Markov problems. In other problems the terminal values must always be supplied as data.

Results

The Dynacode output is shown in Table 4.6. The optimal process from each initial state is given. Where there is more than one initial state Dynacode will give the optimal process from each, unless the statement INITIAL STATE i appears in the program. Here i is the label of an initial state, and the statement causes Dynacode to print the output from the specified initial state only.

In Table 4.6 the section headed OPTIMAL PROCESS FROM INITIAL STATE 1 gives the best sequence of replacement/overhaul decisions for machines which are 1 year old at the start of the planning period. Similarly the section headed OPTIMAL PROCESS FROM INITIAL STATE 2 gives the best sequence for machines initially 2 year's old and so on. From this table we can list the optimal action sequences as shown in Table 4.7.

Table 4.7 Optimal sequence of decisions for each age group

Stage		5	4	3	2	1
Initial age	Size of group					
1	5	overhaul	overhaul	replace	overhaul	overhaul
2	4	overhaul	replace	overhaul	overhaul	overhaul
3	8	overhaul	replace	overhaul	overhaul	overhaul
4	3	replace	overhaul	overhaul	overhaul	replace

Using Table 4.7 we can determine the number of overhauls and replacements in each year. This is shown in Table 4.8.

Table 4.8 Numbers of replacements and overhauls

Stage	5	4	3	2	1
Number of replacements	3	12	5	0	3
Number of overhauls	17	8	15	20	17

Expenditure Analysis

Table 4.6 shows the minimum net present value of expenditure per machine for each age group.

There are initially 5 machines of age 1 and from Table 4.6 we see that the present value of the total costs for each of these machines and its replacements is $25,077. The total cost for the age group is 5 × 25,077 = 25,385. Similar results can be calculated for the other age groups with the results shown in Table 4.9.

Table 4.9 Calculation of the minimum present value of total costs

Initial age	Machines in group	Present value of cost per machine ($)	Present value of cost of group ($)
1	5	25,077	125,385
2	4	27,102	108,408
3	8	34,702	277,616
4	3	7043	111,129
			Total 622,538

The cash flow in each year can be computed by considering the cash flows for each age group.

Consider a machine which is initially of age 1. The optimal sequence of replacement/overhaul decisions for this machine is given in Table 4.6 in the section headed OPTIMAL PROCESS FROM INITIAL STATE 1. At stage 5 the machine is overhauled and from the original data the cost of this is $7000. At stage 4 we have a 2-year-old machine which is overhauled at cost $3000. At stage 3 we have a 3-year-old machine which is replaced at net cost $18,000. At stage 2 we have a 1-year-old machine which is overhauled at cost $7000, and at stage 1 we have a 2-year-old machine which is overhauled at cost $3000. Finally at stage

Table 4.10 Cash flows (undiscounted) for single machines and their replacements ($1000s)

Stage	5	4	3	2	1	0
Initial age						
1	7	3	18	7	3	−2
2	3	18	7	3	9	0
3	9	20	7	3	9	0
4	20	7	3	9	20	−10

Table 4.11 Cash flows (undiscounted) for groups of machines and their replacements ($1000s)

Stage		5	4	3	2	1	0
Initial age	Size of group						
1	5	35	15	90	35	15	−10
2	4	12	72	28	12	36	0
3	8	72	160	63	27	81	0
4	3	60	21	9	27	60	−30
Totals	20	179	268	190	101	192	−40

0 we have a 3-year-old machine which is sold for $2000. The cash flow for the machine initially age 1, and its replacement is as shown in Table 4.10.

Table 4.10 also shows the cash flow per machine per year for machines initially of age 2, 3, and 4, and their replacements.

For the group of 5 machines initially of age 1 the cash flows are simply 5 times those of a single machine. Similar considerations apply to the other groups and give the total cash flows shown in Table 4.11.

CHAPTER 5

Allocation Problems

5.1 General

The decision network method can be applied to problems which involve apportioning a fixed total quantity of a resource, such as money, time, volume, weight, raw material, between a number of competing uses. These are called allocation problems or knapsack problems. An example, which is considered in detail in the next section, is dividing up an advertising budget between a number of media, namely television, newspapers, trade journals, and direct mail advertising. We are assumed to have information about the profit resulting when certain amounts are allocated to each medium. The aim is to allocate the budget so that the total profit is maximized. Constraints restricting the allocations to certain ranges may apply and these can be built into the network. Constraints can be important where, for example, allocations are made yearly and major fluctuations between successive years are to be avoided.

In other applications the resource may be a raw material which can be used to make a number of products. The problem is to allocate a fixed total quantity of raw material to the production of various quantities of several products in such a way that the total profit is maximized. Constraints on the minimum and/or maximum production quantities can be incorporated. An extension of the formulations allows us to vary the amount of raw material available and hence to determine whether additional profit can be generated by buying more or less of the material or by diverting some to another use.

Applications arise where the resource is a fixed volume or weight. The term 'knapsack problem' arises from the situation where a mountaineer wishes to select the most useful set of contents for his knapsack, which has a limited volume. This is equivalent to apportioning a fixed total volume between a number of competing uses. The payoff from carrying a particular quantity of a certain item (e.g., two pullovers) is the utility which the mountaineer associates with that quantity of that item. If one pullover is essential and a fourth pullover is useless then we have a lower limit of 1 and an upper limit of 3 pullovers. The aim in this case is to maximize the total utility of the contents of the knapsack. An extension of the for-

68

mulation enables us to allow for different utilities associated with different total volumes, so that the advantages of a smaller knapsack can be allowed for. The same type of formulation applies if the resource is weight rather than volume. Indeed, we can consider allocation of both weight and volume simultaneously. However, in solving such a problem, all combinations of intermediate levels of weight and volume must be assessed and this may lead to a large network. In addition to the mountaineer's problem, examples arise in the filling of transport containers, in determining aircraft payloads and in provisioning spare parts.

In other applications the resource can be time into which certain activities have to be fitted (e.g., maintenance activities during a shutdown); or footage, frontage or facings in a retail store, allocated to products to maximize profit from sales. Also we have the converse of the budget allocation problem. Instead of achieving maximum profit or utility from a given budget the aim is to achieve a given objective at minimum cost. An example is where a given amount of electrical power generation capacity is to be installed at minimum total cost. The capacity can be provided by building various numbers and sizes of hydroelectric, oil-fired, coal-fired and nuclear power plants. The aim is to allocate the total capacity requirement between the competing fuel sources so as to minimize total costs.

5.2 The Advertising Budget

A company has decided to spend a certain sum on advertising and is considering how to divide the total between four media, television, newspapers, trade journals and direct mail. The profit resulting when various percentages of the budget are allocated to the various media has been estimated for all feasible allocations and these estimates are shown in Table 5.1. Blanks in the table correspond to

Table 5.1 Profit resulting from various advertising budget allocations

| Allocation ($) | Medium | | | |
	Television 1	Newspapers 2	Journals 3	Mail 4
0				20
10				70
20			80	110
30	20	30	110	150
40	110	100		
50	140	160		

allocations which are infeasible or undesirable, for example because existing contracts imply a certain minimum expenditure in certain areas, or because there are limitations on the amount of advertising material which can be prepared in time. For simplicity in this example the total budget is taken as $100 and all allocations are multiples of $10. In a practical case smaller intervals may be taken.

How much of the budget should be allocated to each medium in order to maximize total profits?

Formulation

In the problems considered in earlier chapters the sequential nature of the decision process arose from the fact that decisions were made at successive points in time, for example, decisions about how many vehicles to buy in each year of a planning period. In allocation problems a sequential structure arises if we regard the allocation of the resource to a particular use or product as a stage in the decision process. In the advertising budget problem there are four media and so the decision network has four stages. The order in which the media are considered is unimportant and we shall consider television at stage 1, newspapers at stage 2, journals at stage 3, and mail at stage 4. The state variable is the amount of resource which remains to be allocated, in this case money which remains after some allocations have been made. The intial state will be $100 and the terminal state $0. Any path through the decision network represents a gradually decreasing amount of resource which remains as successive allocations are made. The action variable is the amount of resource allocated to a particular use, in this case the percentage of budget allocated to the current medium. The return variable is the profit generated when a given percentage of budget is allocated to a given medium. The adjacent state is the percentage of budget remaining after the current allocation.

Before giving the complete decision network we shall illustrate the formulation by considering a particular solution to the allocation problem. Let us select some feasible budget allocation, for instance $30 to television, $40 to newspapers, $20 to journals, and $10 to mail. The profit generated by the products for these allocations can be read from Table 5.1. This plan is summarized in Table 5.2 and is shown as a network with a single path in Figure 5.1.

Table 5.2   A feasible budget allocation (not optimal)

Medium (stage)	Money available ($) (state)	Allocation ($) (action)	Profit ($) (return)	Money left ($) (adjacent state)
1 = television	100	30	20	70
2 = newspapers	70	40	100	30
3 = journals	30	20	80	10
4 = mail	10	10	70	0
			Total profit 270	

In Figure 5.1 the top left-hand node represents the initial state where $100 is available for allocation. The arrow leading from this node has action label 30. This represents an allocation of $30 to the medium considered at stage 1, namely television. The profit resulting from this allocation is $20 and is indicated by the

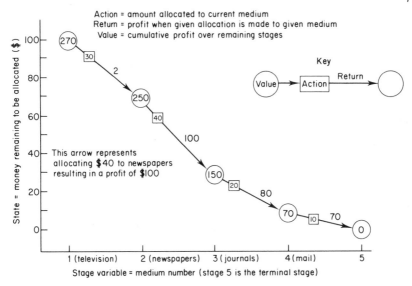

Figure 5.1 Network representation of a solution (not optimal) to the advertising budget allocation problem

return variable shown against the arrow. The adjacent state or end node of this arrow has state variable 70, since $70 remains to be allocated. The next arrow represents allocating $40 to newspaper advertising resulting in a profit of $100. $30 then remains. The next arrow represents allocating $20 to journals for a profit of $80 and the final arrow represents allocating $10 to direct mail for a profit of $70, which completes the allocation. The values entered in the nodes are the cumulative profit at future stages, calculated in a backward pass along the path.

Solution of the Budget Allocation Problem

Figure 5.1 shows how the states, stages, and actions are represented in the decision plane of an allocation problem. Figure 5.2 shows the complete decision network for the problem. The initial state is at top left and represents an initial availability of $100. The arrows labelled 30, 40, and 50 represent allocations of $30, $40, and $50 respectively to the medium considered at stage 1, that is television. The returns from these allocations are $20, $110, and $140 and are shown against the corresponding arrows. If $30 is allocated to television, $70 remains when the next medium is considered. If $40 is allocated then $60 remains when the next medium is considered and so on. Hence the three arrows at stage 1 lead to adjacent states at $70, $60, and $50 remaining budget. Continuing development at the remaining stages yield the complete network shown.

The calculations follow the usual pattern of a backward pass at which the optimal value and action are determined for each state, followed by a forward pass at which the optimal path is identified. The answer to the budget allocation

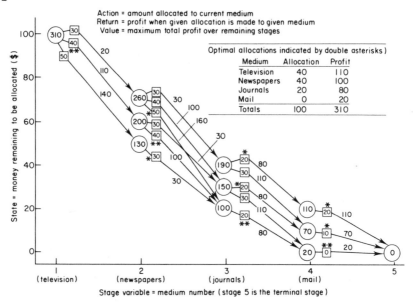

Figure 5.2   Budget allocation: the complete decision network

problem is to allocate $40 to television, $40 to newspapers, $20 to journals and
nothing to direct mail, giving a total profit of $310.

Discussion

In practice the payoff from allocating a given sum to an advertising medium will
not be known accurately. The decision network is an aggregate planning tool
which gives a numerically 'optimal' answer for given data. If this answer differs
widely from management expectations then those expectations are inconsistent
with the data. Either the data or the expectations must be revised.

The decision network emphasizes the interrelationship between the uses to
which the budget is put. This can be achieved by presenting any proposed allocation in the decision network style, for example Figure 5.1. The individual manager
who wishes to increase his share of the total is forced immediately to consider how
to justify the changes he proposes. Without the network the individual manager
tends to be pre-occupied with the fact that increasing his budget share will increase profit from his area. The network highlights the trade-off aspect of budget
allocation and makes it clear that increasing the allocation in one area forces cut-
backs elsewhere which may cause an overall reduction in profit.

Circumstances may allow us to consider increasing or decreasing the total
budget. Such a variation can be introduced into the decision network by having
several states at stage 1 (in terms of Figure 5.2), representing total budgets of
$110, $100, $90, say. The choice of optimal total budget can be incorporated by

adding a stage 0, which precedes stage 1, where actions correspond to determining the total budget. Costs associated with increasing the budget (e.g., extra loan charges) can be incorporated at this stage. A structurally similar procedure is illustrated in the purchasing stage of the problem in the next section.

Finally note that the budget allocation problem can usefully be formulated in terms of allocation *percentages* of a total budget. The $100 total budget considered in the example can be regarded as representing 100% of any actual monetary sum, and the actions and returns can also be regarded as representing various percentages of the same sum. In this way the same formulation can be applied to a range of problems, or to the same problem in successive time periods, with a minimum of modification.

5.3 Purchase and Allocation of a Raw Material

A company can purchase a quantity of raw material at a price indicated in Table 5.3.

Table 5.3   Cost of raw material

Purchase quantity (tonnes)	2	4	6	8
Price ($)	15	28	40	50

The raw material can be used to make products 1, 2, and/or 3 in various amounts with contribution shown in Table 5.4. Because of a contract requirement at least 1 tonne of raw material must be allocated to product 2.

Table 5.4   Contribution from products

Allocation (tonnes)	Contributions		
	Product 1	Product 2	Product 3
0	0	—	0
1	9	6	8
2	18	12	10
3	23	21	11

How much of the raw material should be purchased and how much should be allocated to each product to maximize profits? The profit is given by the total contribution minus the cost of the raw material used.

Formulation and Solution

The formulation and solution are illustrated in the decision network (Figure 5.3). Stage 0 corresponds to buying the raw material and stages 1, 2, 3 to allocating it to products 1, 2, 3 respectively. The state variable is the amount of raw material available for allocation. At stage 0 the action variable is the purchase quantity and

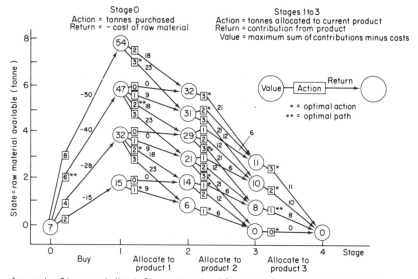

Figure 5.3   Decision network for purchase and allocation of raw material

at the other stages it is the quantity of raw material allocated to the current product in tonnes. The return is minus the cost of raw material at stage 0 and is the contribution of the product at the other stages. The adjacent stage is the amount of raw material available after the current purchase (stage 0) or allocation (stages 1, 2, 3). The state values are the maximum sum of contributions minus costs over the remainder of the decision process. From Figure 5.3 we see that the maximum profit results from buying 6 tonnes of raw material and allocating 2 tonnes to product 1, 3 tonnes to product 2, and 1 tonne to product 3. The profit is then 7 units.

The decision network can be used to study sensitivity to price changes. For example, what price for 8 tonnes of raw material would make that quantity more profitable than 6 tonnes? From the decision network (Figure 5.3) we see that the value of state 8 at stage 1 is 54. This is the maximum total contribution from 8 tonnes of raw material. The profit from 6 tonnes is 7 units, so a price of $54 - 7 = 47$ units for 8 tonnes would make that quantity just competitive and any lower price would make it the more profitable choice. Information of this type is useful to a buyer seeking guidelines for favourable quantity discounts.

5.4 Electrical Generation Capacity

An electricity generating authority plans to install new capacity of 5 GW (gigawatts) of electrical power. The energy sources can be hydroelectricity, oil and/or nuclear. The present value of the cost of installations to produce various capacities from the various sources are as shown in Table 5.5.

Table 5.5   Cost of electricity generating capacity (arbitrary cost units)

Capacity (GW)	Source		
	Hydro	Oil	Nuclear
0	0	0	0
1	2	5	8
2	6	8	9
3	—	10	10
4	—	13	15
5	—	—	17

Dashes in the table indicate capacities which cannot be achieved from the corresponding source. We wish to use the decision network method to represent the possible ways of meeting the capacity requirement and to determine a minimum cost policy.

Formulation and Solution

The decision network is shown in Figure 5.4. The stages correspond to allocating capacity to the different fuel sources. The state variable is the capacity remaining to be allocated. This is 5 GW initially and decreases to zero. The action variable is the capacity to be provided by the fuel currently being considered and the return is the cost of this provision. The minimum cost solution is to generate 4 GW from oil and 1 GW from hydroelectricity at a total cost 15 units.

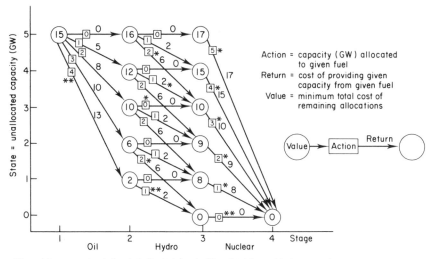

The minimum cost solution is indicated by double askerisks and is to generate 4 GW from oil and 1 GW from hydroelectricity at a total cost of 15 units.

Figure 5.4   Allocation of electrical generating capacity to fuel sources

5.5 Filling a Container—The Knapsack Problem

A container has a capacity of 28 m³ (cubic metres). It can be loaded with varying quantities of any of four different products, labelled products 1, 2, 3, 4. The volume per item of these products is as follows:

Product	1	2	3	4
Volume per item (m³)	12	8	6	2

The expected profits associated with loading various quantities of the products are shown in Table 5.6. To meet commitments at least one of product 1 and 1 of product 3 must be loaded.

Table 5.6   Profit levels

Number of items loaded	Type of product			
	1	2	3	4
0	—	0	—	0
1	22	14	10	2
2	40	28	18	3
3	—	38	26	4
4	—	—	30	5
5	—	—	—	5

How many of each item should be loaded into the container to maximize total profit and what will the profit then be?

Formulation and Solution

This is called a 'knapsack' problem because of the analogy to a mountaineer selecting items to put in a knapsack of limited volume in order to maximize the total utility of the contents. Utility corresponds to profit in the case of filling a container.

A stage corresponds to allocating volume to a product. The stage variable is the product number. In the decision network Figure 5.5, product 1 is considered first and then product 3. This is because there is a requirement to load at least one item of each of these products, which greatly restricts the choices available in the remainder of the network. In fact, it is not possible to load two items of product 1 as this would leave insufficient room for product 3.

The state variable is the volume remaining to be allocated at any stage in the process. The action variable is the number of items of the current product to be loaded. Alternatively one could define the action variable as the volume allocated to the current product. The return is the profit arising from the current product.

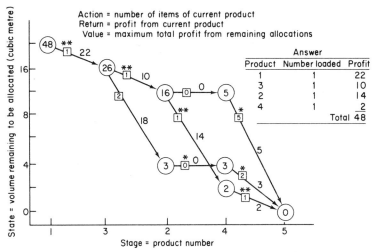

Figure 5.5   Filling a container

Figure 5.5 shows the complete decision network and the solution to the problem.

CHAPTER 6

Progressive Networks, Routeing, and Purchasing Applications

6.1 Progressive Networks

So far we have considered systems whose states fall into groups by stages, so that every path through the network involves the same number of transitions.

The decision network method can also be used for problems which do not have a stagewise structure, provided they satisfy the condition that once the system leaves a given state it can never return to it. Problems of this type are called *progressive* and the associated networks are progressive networks.

The simplest applications of progressive networks arise in routeing problems. The following is an example.

6.2 Gas Supply Problem

Gas supply for a new industrial site can be provided by adding capacity to some sections of an existing network of pipes. The cost of adding capacity to each section is shown in Figure 6.1. A cost of zero indicates that a section already has sufficient capacity. Determine the cheapest way to provide the new supply.

Formulation

The nodes in the gas network (Figure 6.1) are *states* in decision network terminology. The nodes have been numbered and the node number is the *state variable*. A node with no input arrows is an initial state and a node with no output arrows is a terminal state. It is always possible to number a progressive network in such a way that if an arrow goes from state i to state j then i is less than j. To do this, first number the initial state 1 (or 1, 2, 3, etc., if more than one initial state). Then examine the states which can be reached directly from a numbered state until you find one which cannot be reached directly from an unnumbered state, and give it the next number. Continue until all states are numbered. This is called progressive numbering and it has been adopted in Figure 6.1. Progressive

78

numbering of decision networks is not essential, but it has been used here to facilitate description of the computational method.

It is not essential to define an action variable but it is advisable because it makes for easier description of the solution process and makes the formulation

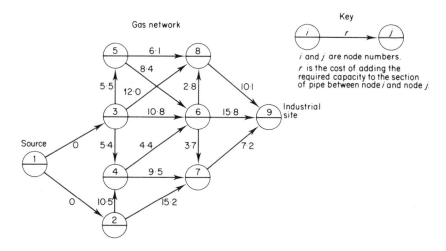

Figure 6.1   Gas supply problem: find the cheapest route through a progressive network

more compatible with stagewise problems. Action j at state i corresponds to the addition of capacity to the section of pipe linking node i to node j.

Calculation

The calculations are similar in principle to those for stagewise networks. There is a backward pass in which the nodes are processed in reverse numerical sequence, that is, highest node first (progressive numbering is assumed here). The optimal value and action are determined for each node. A forward pass is then made to identify the optimal path.

In the gas supply problem the optimal value of a node is the minimum cost of getting the new gas supply from that node to the industrial site. The calculation starts by giving the terminal node, node 9, the value zero. Node 8 is then considered. Only one action is available, namely action 9. In other words, from node 8 the only feasible action is to add capacity to the section from 8 to 9. This costs 10·1 units so node 8 has value 10·1.

Following the reverse numerical sequence, node 7 is processed next. Again only action 9 is available. The cost of this action is 7·2 units and this is the value of node 7.

Node 6 is processed next. The three actions available are to add capacity to sections 6 to 7, 6 to 8 or 6 to 9. The cost of each action is added to the value of its adjacent state (end node) and the action with the smallest total is selected. In detail the calculations are as shown in Table 6.1. The rank column in Table 6.1 indicates the first, second, and third best actions in terms of cheapness.

Table 6.1   The decision at node 6

State (node)	Action (section)	Return (cost)	Adjacent state (end node)	Trial value (total cost)	Rank
6	7	3·7	7	3·7 + 7·2 = 10·9	1*
6	8	2·8	8	2·8 + 10·1 = 12·9	2
6	9	15·8	9	15·8 + 0·0 = 15·8	3

Action 7 has the smallest total cost which is 10·9 units. This is the optimizing action and state 6 has value 10·9 units. This decision is illustrated in Figure 6.2.

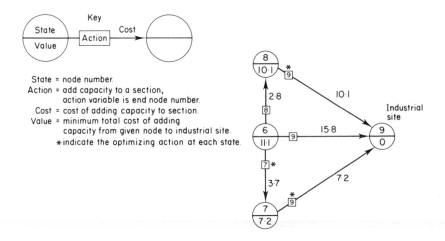

Figure 6.2   Gas supply problem: the decision at node 6

States 5, 4, 3, 2, and 1 are then processed in the same way and this concludes the backward pass. The decision network at the end of the backward pass is shown in Figure 6.3. The optimizing action at each state is marked with an asterisk.

The forward pass starts from the initial state, state 1. The optimizing action (action 3) is identified and its action marked with a second asterisk. This indicates that it lies on the optimal path. We then move along the optimizing arrow to its adjacent state, node 3, where action 4 is found to be optimal. We again mark this with a second asterisk and move forward to the adjacent node. We continue in this way until the terminal node is reached. The complete decision network is shown in Figure 6.4. The cheapest route is nodes 1–3–4–6–7–9 and the total cost is 20·7 units.

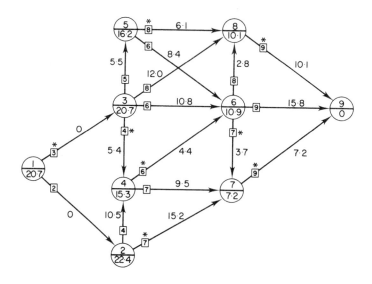

Figure 6.3   Gas supply problem: the decision network at the end of the backward pass

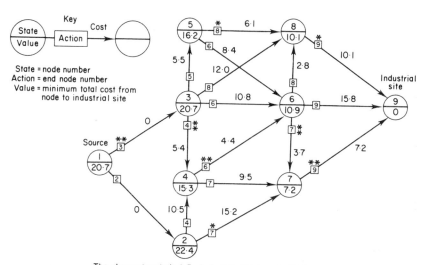

The cheapest route is 1-3-4-6-7-9. Total cost = 20·7.

Figure 6.4   Gas supply problem: the complete decision network

Computer Method Using Dynacode

The Dynacode input for the gas supply problem is shown in Table 6.2. The progressive structure of the problem is indicated by including the statement

Table 6.2   Gas supply problem: Dynacode input

						statement number
DYNACODE GAS SUPPLY PROBLEM						1
LIST INPUT						2
MINIMIZE						3
PROGRESSIVE						4
TERMINAL STATES 1						5
* STATE IS NODE NUMBER						6
* ACTION IS END NODE OF SECTION						7
* VALUE IS MINIMUM REMAINING COST						8
DATA						9
stage	state	action	terminal value or return	adjacent state		
0	9	0	0.0	0	terminal state	10
1	8	9	10.1	9		11
1	7	9	7.2	9		12
1	6	7	3.7	7		13
1	6	8	2.8	8		14
1	6	9	15.8	9		15
1	5	6	8.4	6		16
1	5	8	6.1	8		17
1	4	6	4.4	6		18
1	4	7	9.5	7		19
1	3	5	5.5	5		20
1	3	6	10.8	6		21
1	3	8	12.0	8		22
1	2	4	10.5	4		23
1	2	7	15.2	7		24
2	1	2	0.0	2 ⎫	initial	25
2	1	3	0.0	3 ⎭	state	26
END						27

PROGRESSIVE in the Dynacode program. This is at statement 4 in Table 6.2. The data follow the usual pattern of rows of five numbers, with one row for each terminal state and then one row for each arrow in the decision network. The data follow a backward progressive sequence by state number.

In PROGRESSIVE problems the stage variable serves only to distinguish the terminal, intermediate, and initial states. The stage variable is given the value 0 for terminal states, 1 for intermediate states, and 2 for initial states. For the gas supply problem the state variable is the node number: the action variable is the end node of the relevant section of the gas pipe; the return is the cost of adding capacity to that section; and the adjacent state is the end node of the section. Thus in this formulation it happens that the action and the adjacent state variables are identical.

The data for terminal states consist of the five entries:

(i) 0 (zero), the conventional stage variable for terminal states;
(ii) the state variable (node number);
(iii) a dummy entry usually zero;
(iv) the value of the terminal state;
(v) a dummy entry usually zero.

The data for an action arrow at an intermediate state consist of the entries:

(i) 1, the conventional stage variable for intermediate states;
(ii) the state variable (start node number);
(iii) the action variable;
(iv) the return;
(v) the adjacent state variable (end node number).

For an initial state the only difference is that the stage variable takes the value 2. It is not necessary to use progressive numbering of the states. Any system which assigns a unique number to each state is acceptable.

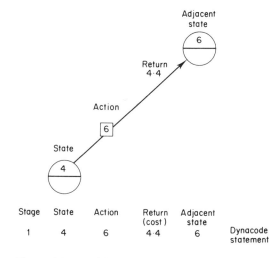

Stage	State	Action	Return (cost)	Adjacent state	
1	4	6	4·4	6	Dynacode statement

Figure 6.5 Decision arrow and Dynacode statement (progressive deterministic problem): the stage variable 1 implies that this is an intermediate state (i.e., not initial or terminal)

Figure 6.5 shows the correspondence between a decision network arrow and its Dynacode data statement. The arrow represents the section of pipe linking node 4 to node 6 and Dynacode statement appears at statement 18 in Table 6.2.

The Dynacode output for the gas supply problem is shown in Table 6.3. This confirms the result found in Figure 6.4.

Table 6.3   Gas supply problem: Dynacode output

DYNACODE GAS SUPPLY PROBLEM
* STATE IS NODE NUMBER
* ACTION IS END NODE OF SECTION
* VALUE IS REMAINING COST
*

STAGE	STATE	ACTION	VALUE
2	1	3	20.7
1	3	4	20.7
1	4	6	15.3
1	6	7	10.9
1	7	9	7.2
0	9	0	0

6.3 Trimloss Problems

In many industries, material such as metal, plastic or wood is purchased in the form of sheets, bars, rolls or planks and then cut to the shape and size required. The cutting process gives rise to scrap, referred to as 'trimloss'. The cost of trimloss is frequently very substantial.

In attempting to reduce trimloss three distinct areas of activity arise. The first is design. The design of the product, the specification of materials, and the detailed instructions for cutting irregular shapes from regular pieces of material require an awareness of trimloss considerations by the designer. The second area is 'linear trimloss'. Linear trimloss is the problem of cutting given numbers of rectangular pieces of given sizes from given numbers of larger rectangular pieces. An example is cutting carpet from rolls with sizes suitable for the rooms, halls, and stairways of a building in such a way as to minimize the total number of rolls used. This problem can best be solved by linear programming. The third area is purchasing. Quantity discounts often arise when material is purchased. For example, for steel bar a substantial discount is obtained by buying a large quantity of one size rather than smaller quantities of each of two sizes. The saving from the quantity discount may be more than the additional cost of trimloss when cutting from the one size. The purchasing problem links in with the general area of stock control and requirements planning.

The decision network method can be useful in analyzing the problem of purchasing items by size so as to minimize material costs, allowing for trimloss and quantity discounts. The example in the next section illustrates this.

6.4 Steel Purchasing

The Problem

A manufacturer makes steel springs to customers orders. The springs are made from bar which is purchased expressly for each order. Because of variations in specification, bar left over from an order is rarely re-usable and is effectively worthless. An order gives rise to a requirement for a number of pieces of bar in various lengths. In the example the lengths range from 2·5 to 4·5 metres in multiples of 0·5 metres. The bar requirements can be met in a variety of ways. If bars were purchased exactly to the length requirements indicated by the designers there would be minimal trimloss. However, the price of bar is subject to discounts which apply when more than a certain minimum amount in pieces of a given length is purchased. The problem is to determine how many pieces of bar of each length should be purchased in order to minimize the total cost.

The Price Structure

The price of bar and the discount structure are as follows. When a given total length of bar is ordered, to be delivered in pieces all of the same length, the cost is

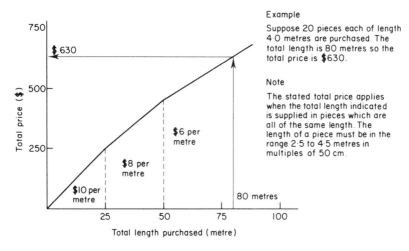

Example

Suppose 20 pieces each of length 4·0 metres are purchased. The total length is 80 metres so the total price is $630.

Note

The stated total price applies when the total length indicated is supplied in pieces which are all of the same length. The length of a piece must be in the range 2·5 to 4·5 metres in multiples of 50 cm.

Figure 6.6   Price of a steel bar

determined by the total length ordered. The first 25 metres cost $10 per metre, the next 25 metres cost $8 per metre and the remainder costs $6 per metre. Thus, if 20 pieces each of length 4·0 metres are ordered the total length ordered is 20 × 4·0 = 80 metres. The first 25 metres cost $10 per metre, subtotal $250. The next 25 metres cost $8 per metre, subtotal $200. The remaining 30 metres cost $6 per metre, subtotal $180. The total cost is $250 + $200 + $180 = $630.

This price structure is presented in the form of a graph in Figure 6.6, which gives the cost of a given total length of bar. The price shown applies when the bar is supplied in the form of pieces all of the same length.

Length Requirements

We consider an order which for minimum scrap requires the numbers of pieces of

Table 6.4   Steel bar requirement

Length of piece (m)	Number of pieces required	Total length at stated size (m)	Cost ($)
2·5	8	20	200
3·0	22	66	546
3·5	14	49	442
4·0	9	36	338
4·5	18	81	636
Grand totals	71	252	2162

bar of the lengths indicated in the first and second column of Table 6.4. This requirement is determined by the design staff and it is assumed that obvious economies like cutting three one-metre sections from a three-metre piece have been allowed for at the design stage.

From Table 6.4 we see that 71 pieces of bar are required in all. There are many ways in which the requirement could be met. At one extreme we could buy the numbers of pieces of each size stated in Table 6.4. Scrap would be nil but so would the quantity discounts. The cost of bar for this solution is shown in the right-hand column of Table 6.4. The total cost is $2162. Five different lengths of bar are purchased. The total length purchased is 252 metres which is the minimum feasible. Note that the cost is not simply the cost of 252 metres with full discount, since discount is lost where less than 50 metres of a given size is purchased.

At another extreme, the requirement could be met by buying all the bar in lengths of 4·5 metres. When a 2·5 metre piece is required we would then take a 4·5 metre piece and cut off 2·0 metres which would be scrap. We assume that there is no possibility of using this scrap because the cutting plan has already been decided by the designers in drawing up the requirements of Table 6.4. Although this solution would cause maximum scrap, it would also ensure maximum discount. The purchase requirement would be for 71 pieces of length 4·5 metres total 319·5 metres. This costs $2067 and is $95 cheaper than the no scrap solution.

Decision Network

Between the two extremes just discussed there are many other solutions involving the purchase of numbers of pieces of various lengths in various combinations. We shall analyze these with the aid of a decision network.

The states of the decision network represent the sizes of bar. The state variable is the piece length in centimetres (centimetres have been used so that the state variable is an integer). An action consists in buying sufficient pieces of bar of a given size to meet the requirements for that size and some smaller sizes, or exceptionally for that size only. The adjacent state is under a given action is the next smaller size which must be purchased. Figure 6.7 illustrates the formulation.

State, i = piece length in centimetres
Action, k = number of pieces of length i purchased, sufficient to meet requirement down to, but not including, length j
Return, r = cost of k pieces of length i
Adjacent state, j = next smaller size purchased under given action
Value, f = minimum total cost of this and smaller sizes

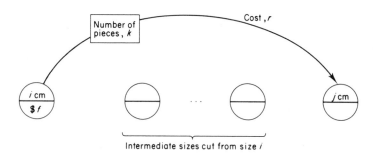

Figure 6.7   Key to decision network

For example, consider the requirement for bar of length 300 centimetres. There are three possibilities:

(i) Purchase no bar of this length, in which case the length, is provided by cutting down a larger size.

(ii) Purchase 22 pieces, i.e., the exact requirement as shown in Table 6.4. The cost of this is $546, determined from Figure 6.6.

(iii) Purchase 30 pieces and use 22 for the 300 centimetre requirement and 8 for the 250 centimetre requirement. This costs $690.

Possibility (i) above is represented by paths in the decision network which do not pass through state 300. Possibilities (ii) and (iii) are represented as shown in Figure 6.8.

In Figure 6.8 the left-hand node represents having sizes of 300 cm and below to consider. Action 22 represents purchasing 22 pieces of this length at cost $546. If

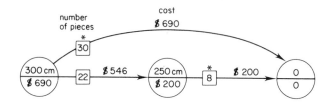

Figure 6.8   The decision relating to 300 cm and 250 cm lengths

this action is taken we shall need to purchase bar of length 250 cm and so this is the adjacent state. Action 30 represents the purchase of 30 pieces of length 300 cm. Since this covers the requirement for 300 and 250 cm the action arrow bypasses state 250. The right-hand node represents a point where all size requirements have been met.

The remainder of the decision network is built up in a similar way. There is an action arrow at each state corresponding to the purchase of sufficient pieces to meet the requirements from that size down to but not including each smaller size.

Table 6.5   Number and cost data

Piece length (cm)	Number of pieces	Total length (m)	Cost ($)
250	8	20	200
300	22	66	546
300	30	90	690
·350	14	49	442
350	36	126	906
350	44	154	1074
400	9	36	338
400	23	92	702
400	45	180	1230
400	53	212	1422
450	18	81	636
450	27	$121\frac{1}{2}$	879
450	41	$184\frac{1}{2}$	1257
450	63	$283\frac{1}{2}$	1851
450	71	$319\frac{1}{2}$	2067

This table shows the possible numbers of pieces of bar of each length which may be purchased and the corresponding cost, determined from the price structure shown in Figure 6.6

Costs for each action determined by reference to Figure 6.6. Table 6.5 summarizes the numbers of pieces of bar purchased under each action and the corresponding costs. Figure 6.9 is the complete decision network. This has been

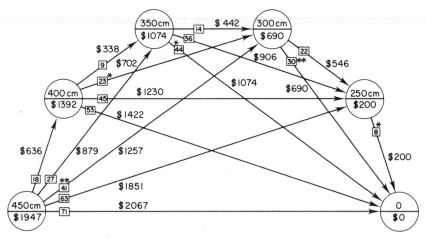

Answer: buy 41 pieces of length 450 cm and 30 pieces of length 300 cm, total cost $ 1947.

Figure 6.9   Steel purchasing: the complete decision network

drawn with the states lying on a semicircle so that the action arrows are straight and a neat layout is obtained.

Result

The usual calculation method is used and the minimum cost solution turns out to be as follows:

buy 41 pieces of length 450 cm, cost $1257
30 pieces of length 300 cm, cost $ 690
_____

Total $1947

The requirement for lengths of 400 and 350 cm will be met by trimming pieces of length 450 cm and the requirement for pieces of length 250 cm by trimming pieces of length 300 cm. This answer strikes the best compromise between trimloss and quantity discounts.

6.5 Algebraic Summary

For progressive problems the definitions and algebra described in Section 2.6 are modified to allow for the fact that there is now no stagewise structure. The algebraic variables are then as follows:

i = state variable
k = action variable
$r(i, k)$ = return associated with state i and action k
j = state adjacent to state i under action k
$f(i)$ = optimal value of state i

The dynamic programming recurrence relation is

$$f(i) = \underset{k}{\text{Max}} \left[r(i, k) + f(j) \right] \tag{6.1}$$

These symbols are summarized in Figure 6.10.

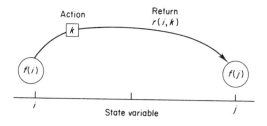

Figure 6.10   Algebraic symbols for progressive networks

CHAPTER 7

Machining, Scheduling, and Sequencing

Introduction

In this chapter we consider some applications of the decision network method to problems in machining, scheduling, and sequencing. It should not be assumed that the decision network method is necessarily the only or even the best method for tackling problems in these areas as a whole. The method is however suited to some problems which have an appropriate structure and the purpose of this chapter is to illustrate some of these.

7.1 Machining Problem—Steel Rolling

Steel initially in strips of thickness 10 cm is to be rolled into strips of thickness 4 cm by passing through up to three rolling stands in succession. The cost of operating a stand depends on the input thickness of the metal and the reduction in thickness required and is shown in Table 7.1. Blanks in the table indicate that the corresponding reduction is technically infeasible. We wish to determine the number of stands to be used and the sequence of reductions which minimizes the total cost of rolling.

Table 7.1   *Steel rolling costs*

Input thickness (cm)	Reduction (cm)		
	1	2	3
10	4	5	8
9	4	6	9
8	4	7	12
7	4	8	12
6	5	10	—
5	7	—	—

Formulation

The input thickness to the first stand is 10 cm and the possible reductions are 1, 2 or 3 cm with costs of 4, 5 or 8 units respectively. The resulting reduced thickness is then the input thickness to the next stand. Figure 7.1 illustrates this. The stage variable is the stand number.

The state variable is the thickness of the steel in centimetres. The action variable is the reduction in thickness at the current stage. At stand 1 this can be 1,

Action = reduction in thickness at this stand, in centimetres
Return = cost of this reduction
adjacent state = thickness at exit from stand (= input thickness for next stand)

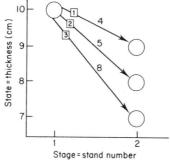

Figure 7.1   Steel rolling problem: the decision at the first stand

2 or 3 cm as shown in Figure 7.1. The resulting reduced thicknesses, 9, 8 or 7 cm, are the possible input thicknesses to stand 2. The return is the cost associated with a given reduction and is determined from Table 7.1. In some applications the return is time rather than cost, the aim being to achieve a given overall reduction as quickly as possible. In this case time, which is relatively easy to measure, acts as an indirect monitor of cost.

The complete decision network is built up by extending the network forward to cover the remaining stands in the manner of Figure 7.1. Figure 7.2 shows this. The cost associated with each possible reduction from given input thickness is determined by reference to Table 7.1.

Solution

Once the decision network has been drawn we carry out the backward and forward pass calculations in the usual manner. The value of a state is the minimum total cost of the remaining reductions. From Figure 7.2 we see that the minimum cost solution is to reduce by 3 cm at stand 1 and by 3 cm at stand 2 for a total cost of 20 units. Stand 3 is not used.

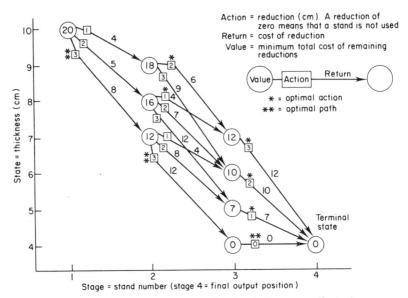

Answer: stand 1, reduce by 3 cm at cost 8; stand 2, reduce by 3 cm at cost 12; stand 3 not used. Total cost 20.

Figure 7.2   Steel rolling problem: the complete decision network

Danglers

In Figure 7.2 only actions which can form part of a plan which achieves the desired overall reduction in three stands or less are shown. For example, at stand 2 with an input thickness of 9 cm it would be technically possible to reduce by 1 cm. The input thickness to stand 3 would then be 8 cm. However, the maximum reduction is 3 cm and hence it would not then be possible to achieve the desired final thickness of 4 cm within three stands. An action corresponding to a 1 cm reduction would have no adjacent state. An action which has no adjacent state is a 'dangler' and cannot be evaluated; it should therefore not appear in the network. Figure 7.3 illustrates this.

In small problems where a complete network is drawn danglers are easy to avoid. In larger problems, or where a basic style of network is used repetitively with varying ranges of stage, state, and action variables, it may be convenient to insert artificial terminal states or actions to which a high cost is given so that the optimal path will not pass through them.

Additional Features

If *exactly* three stands had to be used in the steel rolling problem then the 'zero reduction' which occurs from state 4 at stage 3 would not be allowed. The problem can be solved by deleting state 4 at stage 3, and its input and output arrows, from the network and then performing the usual calculations.

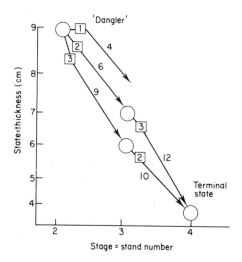

Figure 7.3   A dangler is an action with no
adjacent state

If there is no upper limit on the number of stands then an alternative
progressive formulation can be used. It is also possible simply to extend the
stagewise formulation of Figure 7.2 forward to the maximum feasible number of
stands, that is six. However, the progressive formulation is more compact. It is illustrated in Figure 7.4.

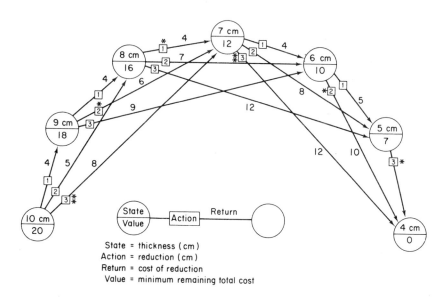

Figure 7.4   Decision network for the steel rolling problem with no limit on the number of
stands used

In the problem described, each stand was assumed to be capable of similar reductions at similar costs. In practice it may be that the operating costs of the stands vary, and so do the range of input thicknesses they can accept and reductions they can achieve. The basic formulation can be adapted easily to cope with these features. In fact, restrictions of this type reduce the size of the decision network and so simplify the solution procedure. Where all stands are identical and the maximum number is limited then zero reductions need only be considered for states at the minimum thickness level. Where the stands are not identical, zero reductions (i.e., bypassing of stands) will need to be considered at intermediate thicknesses.

Finally, note that the model we have developed is applicable in principle to a whole range of machining processes and not just to steel rolling. It can apply to many types of extrusion, cutting, and machining processes. The 'rolling stands' may correspond to a die in an extrusion process, a cutting pass in a turning process, etc. Constraints may arise from the need to make rough cuts initially and finishing cuts at the end of the process.

7.2 Aggregate Production Planning

An aircraft manufacturing company has the orders shown in Table 7.2 for aircraft of a certain type to be completed at the ends of the months indicated. Aircraft can be built in batches of up to four and a maximum stock of three *finished* aircraft can be held at any time. Stock holding is limited by credit restrictions. The cost of building an aircraft varies with the size of the batch in which it is built as shown in Table 7.3.

Table 7.2   Aircraft manufacturers' orders

Month	February	March	April	May	June	July
Aircraft	1	2	5	3	2	1

Table 7.3   Aircraft manufacture costs (millions of $)

Batch size	Cost per aircraft	Cost of batch
1	14·00	14
2	12·00	24
3	11·33	34
4	11·00	44

At the beginning of February one completed aircraft is in stock and existing work in progress is such that three will be completed at the end of February and *not more than* one can be completed at the end of March. Otherwise, completions are at the discretion of the production planner, subject to the constraint that orders are met and that the stock of finished aircraft is zero after the July delivery. Having finished aircraft in stock costs $1m per aircraft per month. This sum allows for cost of work in progress stocks associated with early completion but is regarded as cost being incurred by the finished aircraft. Determine how many aircraft should be completed at the end of each month in order to minimize total costs.

Formulation

In the decision network formulation a stage is a month and the state variable is the number of finished aircraft in stock at the start of a month. Figure 7.5 illustrates the formulation and shows the action arrows for February and March.

At the beginning of February there is one aircraft in stock so the left-hand side in Figure 7.5 is at stock level 1. The action variable is the number of aircraft com-

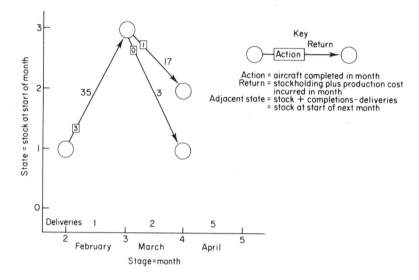

Figure 7.5   Production planning problem formulation and first decision

pleted during the month. We already know that three aircraft will be completed during February. This is represented by the action arrow for that month. One aircraft is delivered in February so the stock at the start of March is three. The cost incurred in February will be (in $ million) 34 units for the completed aircraft plus 1 unit stockholding cost for the stored aircraft, giving a total cost of 35. This is shown against the action arrow for February.

The first decision which the production planner can make relates to March. From existing work in progress we are told that completions in March cannot exceed one, in other words they can be zero or one. Hence two arrows are drawn for March. The arrow for one completion leads to a stock of two next month. The arrow for zero completions leads to a stock of one next month. The adjacent state in each case is derived by calculating the next month's stock level thus:

stock at start of next month = stock now + completions − deliveries

The costs in the current month are given by the sum of the cost of the aircraft completed in the month, determined from Table 7.3, plus the cost of stockholding. Thus for March, with an opening stock of three, if one aircraft is completed the cost is $14 + 3 = 17$. If none are completed the cost is simply the stockholding cost, 3.

Solution

To determine the best production plan we complete the remainder of the decision network as shown in Figure 7.6. The standard calculations are carried out and

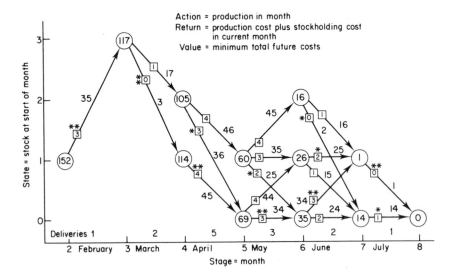

Figure 7.6 Production planning: the complete decision network

yield the optimal path which is indicated by double asterisks. The minimum cost production plan is summarized also in Table 7.4.

Table 7.4 Minimum cost production plan

Month	Completions	Cost in month
2 (February)	3	35
3 (March)	0	3
4 (April)	4	45
5 (May)	3	34
6 (June)	3	34
7 (July)	0	1
		Total 152

Discussion

The analysis just carried out gives the best trade-off between the economies achieved by increasing the batch size and the cost of stockholding. In this type of application the decision network is also particularly valuable in giving a visual representation of the production plan. Stocks, completions, deliveries, and costs appear in a style which helps management to interpret the effects of their decisions and of other changes.

We have referred to this problem as aggregate production planning because it is concerned with planning production of the complete product. In order to finish three aircraft in May, say, it will be essential to produce and buy in many components and to carry out many assembly and test operations well before that time. The detailed planning of these operations will require additional analysis, possibly using other scheduling and sequencing techniques. The decision network method is, however, useful in determining batch sizes in the dynamic situation, as illustrated by the example. More detailed analyses of component production can then be carried out.

The decision network method deals readily with constraints on the stock level and the production rate, provided that the Markov property is retained. This property could break down, for example if the production rate this month could only vary slightly from the rate last month, corresponding to gradual build-up or decline of the production rate. One way of tackling this is to re-define the state variable so that it represents a combination of stock level and production rate. If ten different stock levels and ten different production rates were allowed then there would be 100 states per stage. This is large for manual analysis but not prohibitive when a computer is used.

Additional factors can be built in to decision networks by extending the state and action space, but in practice the art lies in producing a useful model without over elaboration. In most circumstances it is best to abandon the attempt to reflect every nuance of the real situation and to favour a model which is simple to understand and apply. Restrictions on changes in the production rate, for example, can be built in as upper and lower limits on the production rate over a period of six months say. The effect of different limits can be evaluated in a few runs of a simple model. This may prove to be a better approach than developing a model which fully optimizes with respect to production rate.

7.3 Activity Sequencing to Minimize Resource Costs

The Problem

Construction, maintenance, and other projects can frequently be broken down into activities which require resources and may be subject to precedence constraints. In the critical path method the work to be done is broken down to a detailed level so that a project may involve hundreds of activities. Our present concern is with a more aggregate level of planning in which an activity represents something like a block of minor activities (a 'hammock') or a single project in multiproject scheduling.

We consider a set of activities, each of known duration, which must be carried out one at a time. Precedence constraints may apply. Each activity requires expensive resources in known amounts, for example, a crane is hired for the purpose. The hire period for the crane must extend from the first time it is needed until the last time it is needed and the hire charge must be paid even when the crane is not in use. The problem is to sequence the activities so that the total cost of the resources is minimized.

The problem structure and method of solution will be illustrated by a small example. There are four activities, A, B, C, D which must be performed one at a time in some sequence. Activity A must precede activity C. The activities have the durations and require the resources (crane, excavator) indicated in Table 7.5.

Table 7.5   Activity durations and resource requirements

Activity	Duration (weeks)	Resource requirements	
		Crane	Excavator
A	3	1	0
B	1	1	1
C	2	0	1
D	2	1	0

Resource costs: crane $2 per week, excavator $1 per week

Hiring a crane costs (nominally) $2 per week and hiring an excavator costs $1 per week. Once a resource has been hired it must be retained and the hire charge paid, until all the activities which require it have been completed. Determine an activity sequence which minimizes total costs. Activities cannot be split, that is once an activity is started it must carry on until it is finished.

Decision Network

The complete decision network for this problem is shown in Figure 7.8. A state or node represents a set of activities which have been finished. The initial node represents the situation where no activities have been finished and is indicated by the symbol $\emptyset$, the empty set. The terminal node represents the end of the project where all four activities have been finished.

A stage is the carrying out of some activity. The stage variable is the number of activities which have been finished. In the example this goes from 0 to 4. If there were n activities there would be n stages.

An action corresponds to carrying out some particular activity. A detail from the full network is shown in Figure 7.7. State AD represents a point where activities A and D have been finished (in Figure 7.8 two paths lead to this node, representing the possible sequences A,D and D,A). The action arrow represents

State AD =
activities A and D
finished

State ACD =
activities A, C and D
finished

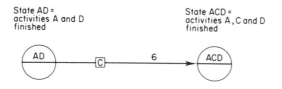

Figure 7.7 Activity C following A and D

carrying out activity C and the adjacent state represents a point where activities A, C, and D are finished. The state labels, e.g., ACD, are written in alphabetical order since they represent a set of completed activities and not the order in which they were finished.

Preceding, Current, and Succeeding Activities

The return associated with an activity is the cost of the resources which are available at the time when the activity is carried out. This includes the cost of resources which are idle as well as those which are in use. The return is determined by examining the resource requirements of:

(i) preceding activities;
(ii) the current activity;
(iii) succeeding activities.

Cost Structure

The costs to be met are:

(a) The cost of resources used by this activity.
(b) The cost of any resources not used by this activity but used by both a preceding and a succeeding activity.

Item (b) is the cost of idle resources and it is the overall total of those costs which will ultimately be minimized.

Example of Figure 7.7

In the case of activity C carried out as in Figure 7.7 the preceding activities are AD and the succeeding activity is B. The costs are as follows:

(a) The cost of resources used by activity C. This is the excavator, used for 2 weeks at $1 per week, cost $2.
(b) The crane is required by a preceding activity and a succeeding activity. It is therefore idle whilst activity C is in progress (for the given sequence). The cost of the idle crane for 2 weeks at $2 per week is $4.

100

The total of the costs under headings (a) and (b) is $2 + $4 = $6, which is the return shown in Figure 7.7. The other costs shown in Figure 7.8 are derived similarly.

Network Structure

Figure 7.8 is built up by starting from the initial node which represents no completed activities. The first activity can be A, B or D. Activity C cannot be first

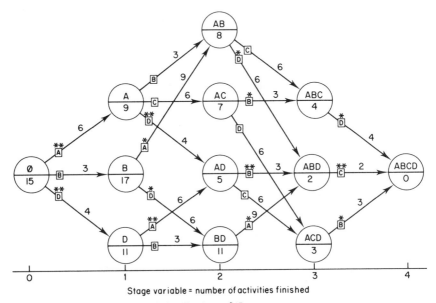

Stage variable = number of activities finished

Answer : sequence A, D, B, C or D, A, B, C. Total cost $ 15.

Figure 7.8   Activity sequencing for minimum resource cost

because it cannot precede A. At stage 1 the three nodes represent completion of A, B, D. If A is finished B, C or D can follow and these lead to nodes AB, AC, AD respectively. From AB we can complete either C or D next, leading to ABC or ABD. Similar development on the other nodes represents the various activity sequences until finally we reach completion of the whole project at node ABCD.

If there are n activities and no precedence constraints the numbers of states at each stage will be in accordance with the coefficients in the binomial expansion. That is, at stage m the number of states will be $n!/m!(n - m)!$. The total number of states will be 2^n. Hence for n greater than about 10 the decision network becomes unwieldy.

Solution

Having completed the decision network structure the usual backward and forward pass calculations are carried out. The answer to the example is to use either of sequences A, D, B, C or D, A, B, C at a total cost of $15. By maximizing over the same decision network we find that the most expensive sequence is B, A, C, D, cost $22. In the minimum cost sequences there is no idle resource cost in this example.

CHAPTER 8

Stochastic Decision Networks and a Marketing Problem

8.1 Introduction

Probabilistic Transitions

The methods described in earlier chapters are applicable to systems where the transitions between state occur deterministically. That is, if a system is in a given state and a given action is taken, then the system moves with certainty to a single, known, adjacent state.

We now consider systems where the transitions between states are probabilistic. For any given state, each action has associated probabilities of transition to each of a number of adjacent states. We assume that the transition probabilities associated with each action are known to the decision maker. For these problems the decision network is modified by the introduction of arrows to represent the transition probabilities, and the calculation procedure is modified by weighting the values of the adjacent states by the probabilities that these states are reached.

Stochastic Networks and the Markov Property

A *stochastic process* is a sequence of random variables. A stochastic network is a network involving probabilistic transitions between states or nodes. The sequence of states visited can be regarded as a sequence of random variables, that is, a stochastic process.

A Markov process is a sequence of random variables in which the distribution of the next random variable depends only on the outcome of the current random variable. In network terms the outcome of the current random variable is the present state of the system and the distribution of the next is the set of transition probabilities from the current state. In a Markov stochastic network the transition probabilities depend only on the current state and action. The decision network method is applicable to Markov stochastic networks. The Markov property for stochastic systems is the same in principle as for deterministic systems (see

Chapter 1, Section 1.2). It can be expressed by saying that the future behaviour of the system must be independent of *how* the current state was reached. In stochastic network terms, the current transition probabilities must be independent of the sequence of states which preceded the current one. Sequential decision problems for which the Markov property holds are called Markov decision problems.

The Markov property is required as a property of the *models* we consider, rather than of the real life systems which they represent. Real systems are subject to many and varied influences and interpretations. A model of a system may be more or less useful depending upon the circumstances. Several different models may be devised to represent any particular system. One extreme form of decision network is the decision tree. This has the property that there is a unique path to each state and in this case the Markov property is not required. Decision trees are discussed in more detail in Section 8.8.

8.2 Stochastic Network Components

In stochastic decision networks actions are represented in the style shown in Figure 8.1. The circle on the left is the present state of the system. An arrow leads

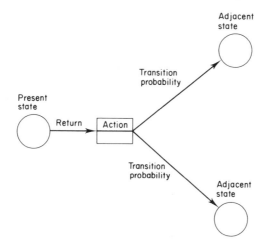

Figure 8.1   An action in a stochastic decision network

to a box which contains the action label in the top half. The bottom half of the box is used to enter the weighted average of the adjacent state values during the calculations. The return associated with this action is written against the arrow. The return is normally a cost, profit, etc. If the returns are really random variables then the mean return is used on the decision network. The calculation procedure maximizes or minimizes the mean total return.

A number of arrows lead from the action box and these represent possible transition to various adjacent states. The transition probabilities are written against these transition arrows. The sum of the transition probabilities associated with any action will be unity. It is possible that some actions may give rise to deterministic transitions in an otherwise probabilistic network. In this case there will be just one transition arrow and the associated probability will be 1.

8.3 Marketing Problem

Outline

The application of the decision network method to stochastic problems is introduced with the aid of the following example.

A company which markets a type of toothpaste is considering how to maximize the profit from the paste, and is examining in detail the forthcoming two-year period 1980–1. The decisions to be made relate to expenditure on advertising, and in particular to two annual advertising contracts. The expenditure on advertising can in reality be set at a number of different levels, but for simplicity we shall assume that only two levels are available, high or low.

The profit from the paste in any year is dependent on the sales volume and the advertising expenditure. The sales volume can vary on a continuous scale which can be approximated by a number of discrete points. For simplicity we shall consider only two sales volumes, high and low.

For a given current sales volume the choice of advertising expenditure for the coming year determines the level of profit in that year (or at least, for modelling purposes it determines the expected profit), and also the probability that sales will be high or low by the start of the following year. The problem is to determine the levels of advertising expenditure, contingent on the actual out-turn in sales volume, which will maximize profits over the two-year period. Allowance must also be made for the value of having high rather than low sales volume at the end of the planning period.

Data

The first decision regarding the level of advertising relates to the year 1980. At the start of 1980 the sales volume is high. If a high level of advertising is chosen the estimated profit generated during the year is (nominally) \$14. If a low level of advertising is chosen the estimated profit generated during the year is \$22. The latter figure is the higher because of the high cost of advertising. The effect of reduced advertising on sales is small in the short term, but is significant by the start of the following year.

A probabilistic forecast of sales volume at the start of 1981 has been made, for both high and low advertising levels in 1980. If high-level advertising is used the probability that the sales are high at the start of 1981 is estimated to be 0·8. The probability that sales are low is therefore 0·2. If low-level advertising is used the probability that sales are high at the start of 1981 is 0·6 and the probability they are low is 0·4.

Forecasts regarding profits and sales at high and low advertising and for high and low initial sales volumes have also been made for 1981 and these are shown in Table 8.1. There is a value of $10 associated with having high rather than low sales volume at the start of 1982. We shall shortly use the data to calculate the best policy, that is, the policy which maximizes the mean total of profits plus terminal value. As a preliminary we first illustrate the decision network representation of the decision for 1980.

Formulation

The decision network representation of the decision in 1980 is illustrated in Figure 8.2.

A stage is a year. The state variable is the sales volume at the start of the year which in our model is either low (state 1) or high (state 2). The action variable is

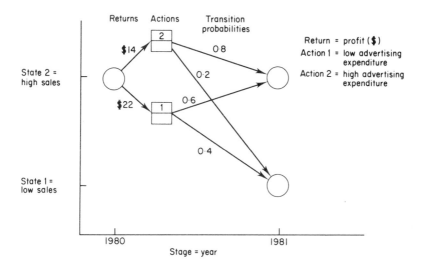

Figure 8.2   Marketing problem: the decision for 1980

the level of advertising expenditure in the current year which coincidentally is also either low (state 1) or high (state 2). The return is the expected profit in the current year which is $22 under action 1 and $14 under action 2. The transition probabilities are 0·4 and 0·6 to states 1 and 2 respectively under action 1 and 0·2 and 0·8 to states 1 and 2 respectively under action 2.

Thus, if action 1 (low advertising) is chosen a profit of $22 will be made this year, the probability of low sales volume at the start of next year is 0·4, and of high sales volume is 0·6. If action 2 (high advertising) is chosen the profit will be

$14 and the transition probabilities 0·2 to low sales and 0·8 to high. The decision network presents this information visually.

Calculations

The data for the marketing problem are summarized in Table 8.1. The decision network prior to the start of calculations is shown in Figure 8.3.

Table 8.1 Marketing problem data

Stage (year)	State (sales)	Action (advertising)	Returns (profit, $)	Transition probabilities	
				to state 1	to state 2
1980	2 ⎰ (high)	1 (low)	22	0·4	0·6
1980	2 ⎱	2 (high)	14	0·2	0·8
1981	1 ⎰ (low)	1 (low)	1	1·0	0·0
1981	1 ⎱	2 (high)	−6	0·5	0·5
1981	2 ⎰ (high)	1 (low)	18	0·3	0·7
1981	2 ⎱	2 (high)	17	0·1	0·9
1982	1 (low)		0 ⎱ terminal values		
1982	2 (high)		10 ⎰		

The calculations are carried out in a backward pass moving from the terminal to the initial states. No forward pass is necessary. We start from the terminal states whose values must be known. In the marketing problem a value of $10 has been associated with having high sales and a value 0 with having low sales at the start of 1982, so the terminal values are 10 for state 2 and 0 for state 1.

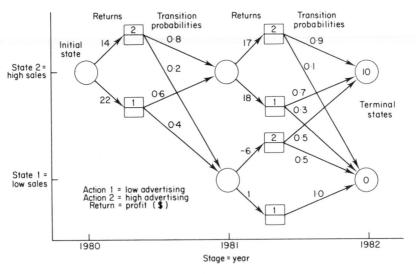

Figure 8.3 Marketing problem: the decision network before calculation starts

Stage 1981 is then considered. Each state is processed in turn. At each state the actions are considered in turn and the value of the mean total future return under each action is calculated. The action which gives the largest value is optimal and is indicated by an asterisk in the action box. The value of the total return under the optimal action is the state value and this is entered in the state node. The mean total future return under a given action is the sum of the return generated at the current stage and the values of the adjacent states multiplied by the probabilities that those states are reached.

We shall describe the calculation in detail for state 2 at stage 1981. The decision network entries are shown in Figure 8.4. Consider action 1 first. To evaluate

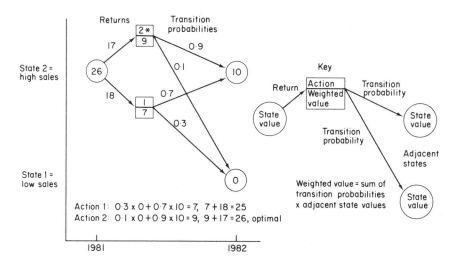

Figure 8.4   Marketing problem: calculation at state 2, 1981

the action we first calculate the weighted value of the adjacent states and enter it in the lower half of the action box. The weighted value of the adjacent states is found by multiplying the value of each adjacent state by the probability of transition to that state and then totalling these products. Under action 1 the probability of transition to state 1 is 0·3 and this state has value 0. The probability of transition to state 2 is 0·7 and this state has value 10. The weighted value is therefore given by

$$0·3 \times 0 + 0·7 \times 10 = 7$$

The weighted value 7 appears in the bottom half of action box 1 in Figure 8.4. The value of the action is the sum of the return, which is 18, and the weighted value, 7, and is 18 + 7 = 25.

Turning to action 2, the transition probabilities are 0·1 to state 1 which has value 0 and 0·9 to state 2 which has value 10. Hence the weighted value is given by

$$0·1 \times 0 + 0·9 \times 10 = 9$$

The value of the action is the sum of the return, which is 17, and the weighted value, 9, and is $17 + 9 = 26$. This is larger than the value of action 1. Action 2 is optimal and this is indicated by a star in action box (Figure 8.4). The state value is 26.

The complete calculations are shown in Figure 8.5. At state 1, stage 1981, the calculations are as follows. For action 1 only one transition is possible and this is to state 1 which has value 0. The weighted value is $1 \times 0 = 0$ and the value of the action is $1 + 0 = 1$. For action 2 the weighted value is

$$0 \cdot 5 \times 10 + 0 \cdot 5 \times 0 = 5$$

and the value of the action is $-6 + 5 = -1$. Action 1 is optimal and value of the state is 1. This concludes the calculations at stage 1981.

For 1980 there is only one state, state 2. Under action 1 the probability of transition to state 1 is $0 \cdot 4$ and this state has value 1. The probability of transition to state 2 is $0 \cdot 6$ and this state has value 26. The weighted value is

$$0 \cdot 4 \times 1 + 0 \cdot 6 \times 26 = 16$$

The return is 22, so the value of the action is $22 + 16 = 38$. Similarly for action 2 the weighted value is

$$0 \cdot 2 \times 1 + 0 \cdot 8 \times 26 = 21$$

and the value of the action is $14 + 21 = 35$. Action 1 gives the larger value and is optimal. The value of the state is 38.

The value of the initial state, 38, is the maximum mean total of profits and terminal values. The optimal plan is indicated by asterisks in Figure 8·5(a) and is shown in Table 8.2.

Table 8.2   Marketing problem: optimal plan

Stage (year)	State (sales)	Action (advertising)
1980	2 (high)	1 (low)
1981	1 (low)	1 (low)
1981	2 (high)	2 (high)

A low level of advertising should be used in 1980. If the sales volume is high at the start of 1981, a high level of advertising should be used in that year, but if the sales volume is low, a low level of advertising should be used.

We see that, unlike the deterministic case, there is no single optimal path through the network. Whichever action we choose in 1980 it is possible for the sales volume to be high or low in 1981. No forward pass calculation is needed. For each state we have an optimizing action which is used contingent on actual arrival in that state.

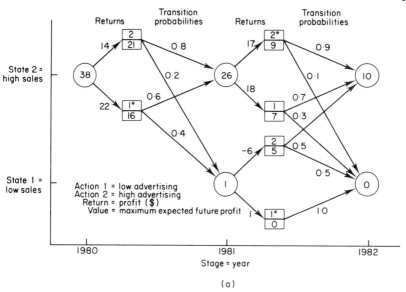

(a)

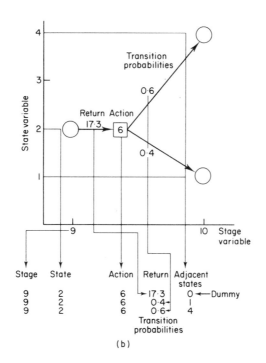

(b)

Figure 8.5 (a) Marketing problem: the decision network with completed calculations. (b) Probabilistic decision network and Dynacode statements

Dynacode

Stochastic decision network calculations can be carried out using the Dynacode computer package. The input for the marketing problem is shown in Table 8.3 and the output in Table 8.4. The statement STOCHASTIC appears in the input. This implies that the network is stochastic and that the data will be in a corresponding stochastic format which is described in the summary of Dynacode in Chapter 14 under the heading Stochastic Action Data. The correspondence between the decision network representation and the Dynacode data statements for probabilistic actions is shown in Figure 8.5(b); the data in this figure are arbitrary.

Table 8.3   Marketing problem: Dynacode input

DYNACODE MARKETING PROBLEM
LIST INPUT
STOCHASTIC
TERMINAL STATES 2
* STAGE IS YEAR
* STATE IS SALES VOLUME 1 = LOW, 2 = HIGH
* ACTION IS ADVERTISING EXPENDITURE 1 = LOW, 2 = HIGH
DATA
1982,1,0,0,0 ⎤
1982,2,0,10,0 ⎦ terminal values
1981,1,1,1,0 ⎤ State 1981, state 1, action 1.   The return is 1 and the
1981,1,1,1,1 ⎦ transition probability is 1 to state 1.
1981,1,2,−6,0
1981,1,2,0.5,1
1981,1,2,0.5,2
1981,2,1,18,0
1981,2,1,0.3,1
1981,2,1,0.7,2
1981,2,2,17,0
1981,2,2,0.1,1
1981,2,2,0.9,2
1980,2,1,22,0 ⎤ Stage 1980, state 2, action 1.   The return is 22 and the
1980,2,1,0.4,1 ⎬ transition probabilities are 0·4 to state 1 and 0·6 to state
1980,2,1,0.6,2 ⎦ 2.
1980,2,2,14,0
1980,2,2,0.2,1
1980,2,2,0.8,2
END

8.4 Discounting

The effect of discounting of future returns on deterministic decision network problems was discussed in Chapter 3. An interest rate of $x\%$ per stage is allowed for by multiplying the state values by a discount factor b, where $b = 1/(1 + x/100)$, at each stage of the calculations. Exactly the same procedure is used in stochastic networks.

Table 8.4   Marketing problem: Dynacode output

DYNACODE MARKETING PROBLEM
* STAGE IS YEAR
* STATE IS SALES VOLUME 1 = LOW, 2 = HIGH
* ACTION IS ADVERTISING EXPENDITURE 1 = LOW, 2 = HIGH
*

BEST ACTION LIST TO RANK 1
*

STAGE	STATE	ACTION	VALUE
1981	1	1	1.000
1981	2	2	26.000
1980	2	1	38.000

END

The output shows the optimal action at each state in backward pass sequence. The state values are also shown. If the statement RANK *k* (where *k* is a positive integer) is included in the input program the output will show the *k* best actions at each state. These will be listed in the order of the value of the actions, where the value of an action is the mean total return generated when that action is used at the current state and optimal actions are used thereafter.

To illustrate the method we shall solve the marketing problem with future returns discounted at $33\frac{1}{3}\%$ per year. The discount factor is then 0·75. The calculations are shown in Figure 8.6. The value of each state is multiplied by the

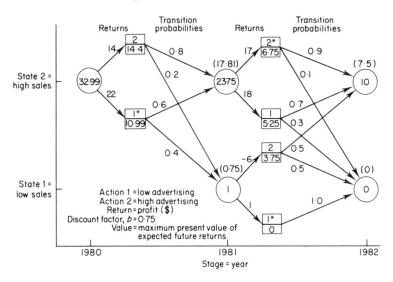

Figure 8.6   Marketing problem with discounting at $33\frac{1}{3}\%$ per year

discount factor before being used to calculate the weighted values. The discounted value of the state is written in brackets above the state node. With the given data and interest rate the optimal actions are unchanged from the undiscounted case. The state values are now the maximum present values of the mean total future returns plus terminal values.

When Dynacode is used to solve a discounted problem the only modification to the input is to include a statement of the form PERCENT x in the program. x is the percentage interest rate per stage. The values appearing on the output table will be the maximum present values of the mean total future returns plus terminal values.

8.5 Algebraic Summary

The method of formulation and the computational procedure for solving stochastic network problems of the type considered in this chapter can be summarized as follows. Let

n denote the stage variable
i denote the state variable
k denote the action variable
j denote the adjacent state variable
$r(n, i, k)$ denote the return associated with stage n, state i and action k
$p(n, i, j, k)$ denote the probability of transition from state i at stage n to state j at stage $n + 1$ under action k
$f(n, i)$ denote the optimal value of state i at stage n

The symbols are illustrated in Figure 8.7.

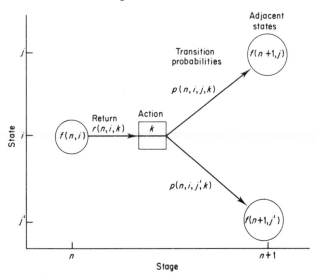

Figure 8.7   Algebraic symbols for a stochastic decision network

The calculation procedure is represented by the following equation, which is the stochastic dynamic programming recurrence relation:

$$f(n, i) = \underset{k}{\text{Max}} \left(r(n, i, k) + \sum_{j} p(n, i, j, k) f(n + 1, j) \right) \qquad (8.1)$$

Equation (8.1) means that the optimal value of state i at stage n is found by choosing the maximum over all actions k of the expression in large parentheses. The expression is the total of the return $r(n, i, k)$ and the summation term, which is the sum of the values of the adjacent states multiplied by the probabilities of transition to each.

For the discounted case the only modification required is multiplication of the adjacent state values by the discount factor $b \geqslant 0$ so that the equation becomes

$$f(n, i) = \underset{k}{\text{Max}} \left(r(n, i, k) + b \sum_j p(n, i, j, k) f(n + 1, j) \right) \qquad (8.2)$$

The calculation proceeds in a backward recurrence (backward pass) form from known terminal values $f(t, i)$.

8.6 Decision Trees

A technique which is already well documented is the method of decision trees (for example Mitchell 1972, p. 78). In graph theory a 'tree' is a network in which

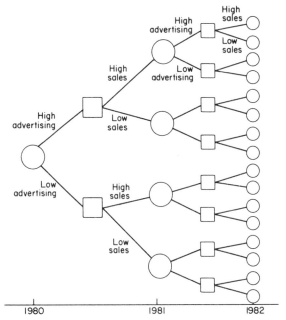

Figure 8.8   Decision tree for the marketing problem: the corresponding decision network representation is given in Figure 8.3

there is exactly one path between any pair of nodes. A decision tree is a special case of a decision network, in which the network is a tree. Because every state in a decision tree is reached by a unique path the Markov property is no longer required. A decision tree is an extreme form of decision network in which no advantage is taken of the possible independence of the current state from the exact sequence of preceding actions. Where such independence exists the decision tree formulation is inefficient. Where such independence does not exist the decision network and decision tree techniques are identical.

A difficulty with decision trees is that the number of nodes grows exponentially with the number of stages. Figure 8.8 shows the decision tree representation of the marketing problem.

The corresponding decision network representation is shown in Figure 8.3. In the decision network there are only two states in 1981 and two in 1982. In the decision tree there are four states in 1981 and sixteen in 1982. Extension by a few addition stages would lead to absurd numbers of states in the decision tree, whilst the decision network would remain at two states per stage.

CHAPTER 9

Dynamic Stock Control

9.1 Dynamic Stock Control Models

Stock control is an important practical problem in industry. It has many features, including stock recording, demand forecasting, and the determination of re-order levels and order quantities. The determination of re-order levels and order quantities will concern us in this chapter. Most of the substantial literature on stock control problems is concerned with determining re-order policies on the assumption that either the demand is constant or that the demand is a random variable with a distribution that does not vary with time. Dynamic stock control, by contrast, is concerned with the determination of re-order policies in a situation where the demand distribution may vary from period to period over a limited planning horizon.

Stock control situations are subject to a large number of variations relating to such factors as how frequently the stock level is reviewed, the length of the lead time between order and delivery and whether backlogging of orders is allowed. The purpose of this chapter is not to present an extensive coverage of these features, but to show how the decision network method can be adapted to exploit the special structure of stock control problems. The technique is described with the aid of an example.

9.2 Butane Stock Problem

A camp site operator sells cylinders of butane gas used for cooking, etc. He visits a town once a month and can purchase cylinders for $10 each from a wholesaler. He estimates that it costs him $5 per visit to the wholesaler for transport and time. Storage costs $1 per cylinder per week or part of a week. The cylinders sell at $18 each. The demand for cylinders varies with the time of year and is probabilistic. The camping season lasts three months and the demand probabilities for each month are shown in Table 9.1. Demand which is not immediately satisfied is lost. Cylinders remaining at the end of the season are valued at $8 each. The operator wishes to determine a replenishment plan which maximizes his expected total profit over the season.

Table 9.1   Butane stock problem: demand probabilities

Demand	Month		
	December	January	February
0			0·5
1	0·3	0·3	0·4
2	0·4	0·3	0·1
3	0·3	0·4	

Formulation

A month is a stage in the decision network and the stage variable is the month number (December $= 12$, January $= 1$, February $= 2$). The state variable is the stock level at the start of the month, just before the operator visits the town (we assume that visits occur at the start of each month). The state variable will be denoted by the symbol i.

An action, k, consists in purchasing sufficient cylinders to bring stock up to level k. The stock level immediately after a purchase is called the *replenished stock level*. If the stock before purchase was i and the replenished stock level is k then the purchase quantity is $i - k$. The expected profit generated in a month is given by the expected income from sales minus the purchase and storage costs. The transition probabilities are determined by the various sales probabilities. The value of a state is the maximum total expected future profit plus terminal values from that state. The value of an action is total expected future profit plus terminal values when that action is used at the current state and optimal actions are used thereafter.

We can reduce the amount of calculation by realizing that:

(a) the situation after purchase depends only on the replenished stock level;
(b) the probabilities of selling 0,1,2, etc., items act as weights for both the sales income and the adjacent state values.

To exploit features (a) and (b) above we use the non-standard decision network indicated in Figure 9.1. The returns are split into two components. The first component, denoted c in Figure 9.1, is the purchase cost and this is handled in the standard way. The second component is the storage cost and income from sales. The calculation of this component is linked with the calculation of the weighted value of the adjacent states. The modified weighted value, w, is given by

$$w = -\text{storage cost} + \text{weighted sum of sales income and adjacent state values}$$

Inventory theory shows that the solution to the problem will have a special structure. There will be a certain stock level before replenishment, referred to as the

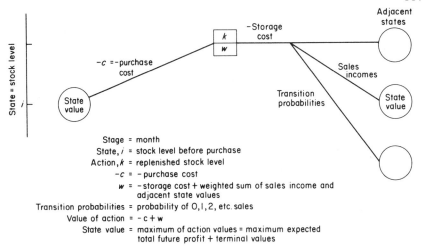

Figure 9.1   Butane stock problem: summary of formulation

safety stock and a certain stock level after replenishment, called the *critical replenished stock level* which will have the following properties:

> If stock is at or above the safety stock buy none.
> Otherwise buy enough to bring stock up to the critical replenished stock level.

This is called an S,s policy, where S denotes the critical replenished stock level and s denotes the safety stock. In dynamic stock control the values of S and s will vary from stage to stage. The structure of the S,s policy is exploited by carrying out the calculations at each stage in the following sequence:

(i) Consider stock level 0. Consider replenished stock levels $k = 0,1,2$, etc., in sequence. We can assume that the values of these actions will increase up to the optimum and then decrease. Hence if the value of action $k + 1$ is less than the value of action k then k is the critical replenished stock level.

(ii) Consider stock levels $i = 1,2,3$, etc., in sequence. The optimal action will be either to purchase enough to bring the stock up to the critical replenished stock level or to purchase none. The smallest stock level at which the optimal purchase quantity is zero is the safety stock s. For $i \geqslant s$ the optimal purchase quantity will be zero.

We illustrate the procedure by solving the butane stock problem.

Calculations: February

The decision network for February is shown in Figure 9.2 and the detailed calculations are given in Table 9.2. The terminal states are the possible stock

Table 9.2 Calculations at stage 2: February

Row	State = stock before replenishment i	Action = stock after replenishment k	−purchase cost $-c$	−storage cost + sum of sales income and adjacent state value weighted by sales probabilities w	Value of action * = optimal $-c + w$
1	0	0	0	0	0*
2	0	1	−15	$-1 + 0.5(0 + 8) + 0.5(18 + 0) = 12$	$-15 + 12 = -3$
3	1	1	0	as for row 2	$0 + 12 = 12$*
4	$i \geqslant 2$	i	0	$-i + 0.5(0 + 8i) + 0.4[18 + 8(i-1)] + 0.1[36 + 8(i-2)] = 6 + 7i$	$6 + 7i$*

levels at the beginning of March. The cylinders are worth $8 each at the beginning of March so a stock level of i cylinders has value $8i$.

We start the calculation by considering the situation where the stock level is zero at the beginning of February. We consider replenished stock levels $k = 0,1,2$ ... in increasing sequence. We can assume that the state value will increase with k up to a certain point and then decrease. Hence, if the value of action $k + 1$ is less than the value of action k then action k is optimal. The steps in the calculation will be explained by reference to Table 9.2.

Table 9.2, Row 1:
    State = stock before replenishment = 0
    Action = replenished stock level = 0
    Purchase cost = 0
    Storage cost = 0
    Probability $1 \cdot 0$ of 0 cylinders sold and adjacent state value 0
    Value of action = 0

Row 2:
    State = stock before replenishment = 0
    Action = replenished stock level = 1
    1 cylinder purchased at cost $15 (including transport and time)
    1 cylinder stored at cost $1
    Probability $0 \cdot 5$ of 0 cylinders sold and adjacent state value 8
    Probability $0 \cdot 5$ of 1 cylinder sold and adjacent state value 0
    Value of action = -3

Hence the value of action 1 is less than the value of action 0 and the critical replenished stock level is 0. No further actions need be considered. Also the safety stock is zero and the optimal purchase quantity is zero for all states.

Row 3:
    State = stock before replenishment = 1
    Action = replenished stock level = 1 (optimal)
    0 cylinders purchased, purchase cost = 0
    Storage and probability terms as row 2
    State value = 12

Row 4:
    State = stock before replenishment = $i \geqslant 2$
    Action = replenished stock level = i (optimal)
    0 cylinders purchased, purchase cost = 0
    i cylinders stored at cost $$i$
    Probability $0 \cdot 5$ of 0 cylinders sold and adjacent state value $8i$
    Probability $0 \cdot 4$ of 1 cylinder sold and adjacent state value $8(i - 1)$
    Probability $0 \cdot 1$ of 2 cylinders sold and adjacent state value $8(i - 2)$
    State value = $6 + 7i$

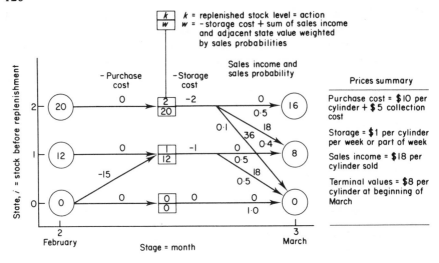

k = replenished stock level = action
w = $-$ storage cost + sum of sales income and adjacent state value weighted by sales probabilities

Figure 9.2   Butane stock problem: decision network for February

Row 4 of Table 9.2 deals with stock levels of 2 or more cylinders before replenishment. For all such states the optimal purchase quantity will be zero and hence the stock level after replenishment will also be i. The storage cost will be $-\$i$. The probability of selling no cylinders will be 0·5 and if that occurs there will be zero sales income and the adjacent state will be at stock level i and hence will have value $8i$. If 1 cylinder is sold, which occurs with probability 0·4, the sales income will be \$18 and the adjacent state will be at stock level $i-1$ and will have value $8(i-1)$. Similarly, with probability 0·1 there will be 2 cylinders sold for \$36 and the adjacent state will be at stock level $i-2$ with value $8(i-2)$. The total expected value computes to $6+7i$. This formula gives us the value of all states $i \geqslant 2$. For example, for $i=2$ the value is $6+7 \times 2 = 20$ and for $i=3$ it is $6+7 \times 3 = 27$.

In summary, the calculations for February yield the results that no cylinders should be purchased and give the values of various stock levels at the beginning of February as shown in the nodes on the left of Figure 9.2. For stock levels of $i=2$ or more the values are $6+7i$.

Calculations: January

The decision network for January is shown in Figure 9.3 and the detailed calculations are given in Table 9.3. The state values on the right of Figure 9.3 are carried over from the left of Figure 9.2, with extrapolation using the formula $6+7i$ for values of states $i \geqslant 2$.

The calculation starts from a stock level of zero at the beginning of January

Table 9.3 Calculations at stage 1: January

Row	State = stock before replenishment i	Action = stock after replenishment k	−purchase cost $-c$	−storage cost + sum of sales income and adjacent state value weighted by sales probabilities w	Value of action * = optimal $-c + w$
1	0	0	0	0	0
2	0	1	−15	$-1 + 1 \cdot 0(18 + 0)$ $= 17$	$-15 + 17 =$ 2
3	0	2	−25	$-2 + 0 \cdot 3(18 + 12) + 0 \cdot 7(36 + 0)$ $= 32 \cdot 2$	$-25 + 32 \cdot 2 =$ 7·2
4	0	3	−35	$-3 + 37 \cdot 8 + 0 \cdot 3 \times 20 + 0 \cdot 3 \times 12 + 0 \cdot 4 \times 0 = 44 \cdot 4$	$-35 + 44 \cdot 4 =$ 9·4*
5	0	4	−45	$-4 + 37 \cdot 8 + 0 \cdot 3 \times 27 + 0 \cdot 3 \times 20 + 0 \cdot 4 \times 12 = 52 \cdot 7$	$-45 + 52 \cdot 7 =$ 7·7
6	1	1	0	as for row 2	$0 + 17 =$ 17
7	1	3	−25	as for row 4	$-25 + 44 \cdot 4 =$ 19·4*
8	2	2	0	as for row 3	$0 + 32 \cdot 2 =$ 32·2*
9	2	3	−15	as for row 4	$-15 + 44 \cdot 4 =$ 29·4
10	3	3	0	as for row 4	$0 + 44 \cdot 4 =$ 44·4*
11	4	4	0	as for row 5	$0 + 52 \cdot 7 =$ 52·7*
12	$i \geqslant 5$	i	0	$-i + 37 \cdot 8 + 0 \cdot 3[6 + 7(i-1)] + 0 \cdot 3[6 + 7(i-2)]$ $+ 0 \cdot 4[6 + 7(i-3)] = 29 \cdot 1 + 6i$	$29 \cdot 1 + 6i$*

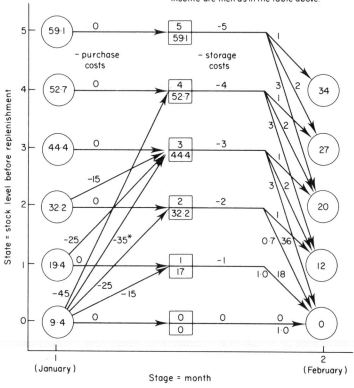

Sales data

Number sold	Probability	Income
I	0·3	18
2	0·3	36
3	0·4	54

Where numbers 1,2,3 appear
against transition arrows these
are the numbers of cylinders sold.
Transition probabilities and sales
income are then as in the table above.

Figure 9.3   Butane stock problem: decision network for January

and replenished stock levels $k = 0,1,2,3,4$ are considered in sequence. We shall
detail the steps in the calculations of Table 9.3 for selected rows only:

Table 9.3, Row 3:
    State = stock before replenishment = 0
    Action = stock after replenishment = 2
    2 cylinders purchased at cost \$25
    2 cylinders stored at cost \$2
    Probability 0·3 of 1 cylinder sold and adjacent state value 12
    Probability 0·7 of 2 cylinders sold and adjacent state value 0
    Value of action = 7·2

Row 4:

 State = stock before replenishment = 0
 Action = stock after replenishment = 3
 3 cylinders purchased at cost $35
 3 cylinders stored at cost $3
 Probability 0·3 of 1 cylinder sold yielding $18
 Probability 0·3 of 2 cylinders sold yielding $36
 Probability 0·4 of 3 cylinders sold yielding $54
 Expected sales income is $0·3 \times 18 + 0·3 \times 36 + 0·4 \times 54 = \$37·8$, only this
  final figure is shown in Table 9.3. The expected sales income is calculated
  separately because it applies to all replenished stock levels of 3 or more
 Probability 0·3 of adjacent state value 20
 Probability 0·3 of adjacent state value 12
 Probability 0·4 of adjacent state value 0
 Value of action = 9·4

Continuing to row 5 shows that the maximum value of state 0 occurs when the replenished stock level is 3, so this is the critical replenished stock level. The state value is 9·4.

Having determined the critical replenished stock level we consider states 1,2,3, etc. The optimal action will be either to buy none or to buy enough to bring the stock up to the critical replenished stock level. Rows 6 and 7 of Table 9.3 show the calculation at state 1:

Table 9.3, Row 6:

 State = stock before replenishment = 1
 Action = stock after replenishment = 1
 Purchase cost = 0
 Storage and probability terms as for row 2
 Value of action = 17·0

Row 7:

 State = stock before replenishment = 1
 Action = stock after replenishment = 3
 2 cylinders purchased at cost $25
 Storage and probability terms as for row 3
 Value of action = 19·4*

Buying none has value 17·0 and bringing the stock up to the critical replenishment level has value 19·4. It is therefore optimal to bring the stock up to the critical replenishment level. State 1 is therefore below the safety stock level. Note that we have been able to use the storage and probability terms, w, from rows 2 and 3 in the calculations at rows 6 and 7. This economy and the restriction to only two actions under the S,s policy make the calculations simple at states other than state 0.

Continuing to state 2, we find, in rows 8 and 9 of Table 9.3, that the optimal purchase quantity is zero and therefore 2 is the safety stock. For stock levels $i > 2$

Table 9.4 Calculations at stage 12: December

Row	State = stock before replenishment i	Action = stock after replenishment k	−purchase cost $-c$	−storage + sum of sales income and adjacent state value weighted by transition probabilities w	Value of action * = optimal $-c + w$
1	0	0	0	$1\cdot0(0 + 9\cdot4) = 9\cdot4$	$0 + 9\cdot4 = 9\cdot4$
2	0	1	−15	$-1 + 1\cdot0(18 + 9\cdot4) = 26\cdot4$	$-15 + 26\cdot4 = 11\cdot4$
3	0	2	−25	$-2 + 0\cdot3(18 + 19\cdot4) + 0\cdot7(36 + 9\cdot4) = 41\cdot0$	$-25 + 41\cdot0 = 16\cdot0$
4	0	3	−35	$-3 + 36 + 0\cdot3 \times 32\cdot2 + 0\cdot4 \times 19\cdot4 + 0\cdot3 \times 9\cdot4 = 53\cdot2$	$-35 + 53\cdot2 = 18\cdot2$
5	0	4	−45	$-4 + 36 + 0\cdot3 \times 44\cdot4 + 0\cdot4 \times 32\cdot2 + 0\cdot3 \times 19\cdot4 = 64\cdot0$	$-45 + 64\cdot0 = 19\cdot0$
6	0	5	−55	$-5 + 36 + 0\cdot3 \times 52\cdot7 + 0\cdot4 \times 44\cdot4 + 0\cdot3 \times 32\cdot2 = 74\cdot2$	$-55 + 74\cdot2 = 19\cdot2*$
7	0	6	−65	$-6 + 36 + 0\cdot3 \times 59\cdot1 + 0\cdot4 \times 52\cdot7 + 0\cdot3 \times 44\cdot4 = 82\cdot1$	$-65 + 82\cdot1 = 17\cdot1$
8	1	1	0	as for row 2	$0 + 26\cdot4 = 26\cdot4$
9	1	5	−45	as for row 6	$-45 + 74\cdot2 = 29\cdot2*$
10	2	2	0	as for row 3	$0 + 41\cdot0 = 41\cdot0*$
11	2	5	−35	as for row 6	$-35 + 74\cdot2 = 39\cdot2$

the optimal purchase quantity will be zero. Rows 10 and 11 show the evaluation of states 3 and 4 with zero purchase quantity. For $i \geqslant 5$ the adjacent state values increase linearly and this allows us to get an algebraic form for the state values in January. The value of state i is $29 + 6i$, $i \geqslant 5$.

The calculations for January are now complete. The critical replenished stock level is 3 and the safety stock is 2. The camp site operator should buy no cylinders if his stock is 2 or more. Otherwise he should buy enough to bring his stock to 3.

Calculations: December

The calculations for December are shown in Table 9.4. Figure 9.4 shows the decision network relating to the decision at stock level zero. This yields the result that the critical replenished stock level is 5. Figure 9.5 shows the determination of the safety stock level. This has been drawn separately to avoid overcrowding Figure 9.4.

In Table 9.4, rows 1 to 7 show the calculations at state 0, that is those corresponding to the determination of the critical replenished stock level. Rows 8 and 9 relate to state 1 and show that the purchase quantity there should bring stock up to the critical level. Rows 10 and 11 relate to state 2 and show that the optimal purchase quantity there is zero. Hence, 2 is the safety stock. All these calculations are similar in principle to those for January.

We conclude that for December the safety stock is 2 and the critical replenished stock level is 5. The camp site operator should buy no cylinders if his stock is 2 or more; otherwise he should buy enough to bring his stock to 5.

Optimal Policy

The answer to the butane stock problem is summarized in Table 9.5. In each month the purchase quantity should be zero if the initial stock is greater than or equal to the safety stock. Otherwise the purchase quantity should be sufficient to bring the stock up to the critical replenished stock level.

Table 9.5   Butane stock problem: answer

Month	December	January	February
Safety stock	2	2	0
Critical replenished stock level	5	3	0

9.3 Algebraic Summary

The formulation of the butane stock problem can be summarized algebraically as follows. Let

n = month number
i = stock level before replenishment (state), $i \geqslant 0$

126

Sales data

Number sold	Probability	Income
1	0·3	18
2	0·4	36
3	0·3	54

Where numbers 1,2,3 appear against
transition arrows these are the
numbers of cylinders sold.
Transition probabilities and sales income
are then as in the table above.

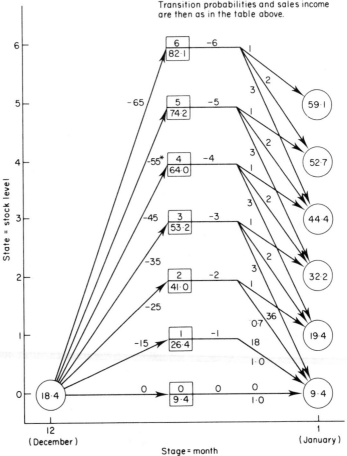

Figure 9.4   Butane stock problem: decision network showing determination of the critical replenished stock level for December

k = stock level after replenishment (action), $k \geqslant i$

$c(k - i)$ = cost on buying $k - i$ cylinders

$h(k)$ = storage cost of k cylinders per month or part of a month

x = number of cylinders sold, $x \geqslant 0$

$t(x)$ = income from selling x cylinders

$q(n, x, k)$ = probability of selling exactly x cylinders in month n, given that the stock level after replenishment is k. $q(n, x, k)$ is the probability that the demand is x, unless $x = k$ when it is the probability that the demand is greater than or equal to x

$f(n, i) =$ maximum expected total profit plus terminal values given stock i before replenishment at the start of month n

$w(n, k) =$ maximum expected total profit plus terminal values given stock k after replenishment at the start of month n

$f(3, i) =$ value of i cylinders at the beginning of March (terminal values given)

$k_n^* =$ critical replenished stock level at stage n

$i_n^* =$ safety stock at stage n

Safety stock = lowest stock level for which the optimal purchase quantity is zero
In this case the safety stock is 2.

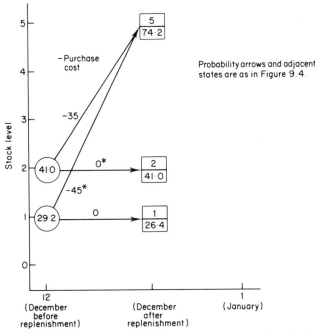

Figure 9.5   Butane stock problem: determination of the safety stock for December

The computations use the following recursive equations:

$$w(n, k) = -h(k) + \sum_{x=0}^{k} q(n,x,k)[t(x) + f(n-1, k-x)] \qquad (9.1)$$

$$f(n, 0) = \max_{k} [-c(k) + w(n, k)] \qquad (9.2)$$

The optimizing value of k in equation (9.2) is the critical replenished stock level, k_n^*. That is,

$$f(n, 0) = -c(k_n^*) + w(n, k_n^*) \qquad (9.3)$$

Having used equations (9.1) and (9.2) to determine the critical replenished stock level we determine the safety stock i_n^*, as follows:

$$i_n^* = \text{smallest } i \text{ such that } w(n, i) \leqslant -c(k_n^* - i) + w(n, k_n^*) \tag{9.4}$$

For $i < i^*$

$$f(n, i) = -c(k_n^* - i) + w(n, k_n^*) \tag{9.5}$$

For $i \geqslant i^*$

$$f(n, i) = w(n, i) \tag{9.6}$$

Equations (9.4) through (9.6) can also be summarized in the single equation

$$f(n, i) = \text{Max}[w(n, i) : -c(k_n^* - i) + w(n, i^*)], \quad i \geqslant 1 \tag{9.7}$$

The colon on the right-hand side of equation (9.7) is read as 'or'.

The result of the analysis is a month by month sequence of control variables k_n^*, i_n^*, which are the critical replenishment level and safety stock at month n. These are equivalent to the variables S,s of inventory policies.

9.4 Computational Aspects of Dynamic Stock Control

The solution of the dynamic stock control problem which has just been given involves a total to about 100 additions or multiplications. These steps would take under one second in a computer.

If the problem were larger, the computational burden would increase linearly with the number of stages, linearly with the number of states per stage and linearly with the number of possible items sold per month. It may appear from this that the amount of computation would soon become prohibitive. However, it is rarely necessary in practice to divide the stock level into more than about ten ranges. These may, for example, correspond to stock levels of 0–100, 101–200, 201–300 items, etc. Similarly, the sales levels can be restricted to, say, three ranges, corresponding to high, medium, and low sales. The accuracy of forecasting is unlikely to justify detailed calculations for more than twelve periods ahead.

From the foregoing analysis it follows that the computations involved in solving a problem of realistic size are of the order of 1000 additions and multiplications. This puts the technique well within the range of feasibility when a computer is used, even when there are many product lines to consider.

Whilst general purpose packages such as Dynacode can be of assistance in dynamic stock control, the special structure of these problems means that it is better to develop purpose-built programs for this application.

CHAPTER 10

Markov Decision Processes

10.1 Introduction

The techniques described in Chapter 1 to 9 apply to networks with a finite number of stages. In practice this means something like annual decision making over a five-year planning period, monthly decisions over a period of one or two years, and so on. The data in such problems usually vary from stage to stage, though the methods are equally valid when the data remain unchanged. Problems where the data are the same at every stage are said to have *stationary data*. An example of such a problem has already been given in Section 4.7.

Many real systems have data which are stationary, or at least can be regarded as stationary for planning purposes, and operate with no clear end point or break point in view. It is useful, therefore, to have models for sequential decision problems with remote planning horizons, and these will be discussed in the remainder of this book. It is worth noting that many mathematical models and formulae such as the square root formulae in stock control, queueing formulae, replacement models and most linear programming models give steady-state solutions to problems, so that mathematically speaking, steady-state solutions are the rule rather than the exception.

Systems which make a sequence of probabilistic transitions, in which the transition probabilities depend only on the current state of the system are said to undergo a *Markov process*. If such a system generates returns at each stage then it is called a *Markov process with returns*. If, in addition, there are alternative actions amongst which a choice can be made then this is a *Markov decision process*. The problems considered in Chapters 8 and 9 were Markov decision processes with non-stationary data (the returns and transition probabilities varied from stage to stage) and with finite planning horizons.

10.2 A Markov Process with Returns

Hiring a Secretary

A man employs a secretary who may resign at the end of any month. When a secretary leaves a temporary is employed on a contract which is renewable monthly and the man advertises for another regular secretary. The probability that a regular secretary resigns in any month is 0·2 and the probability of the secretary remaining in the post is 0·8. When a temporary is employed the probability of finding a regular secretary in any month is 0·7, and the probability of having a temporary again the following month is 0·3. The cost of a regular secretary is $300 per month and the cost of a temporary is $430 per month. What is the average cost per month?

Formulation

We can represent the problem as a system in which state 1 corresponds to having a regular secretary and state 2 to having a temporary. If there is a regular secretary (state 1) in the current month the cost is $300 the probability of having a

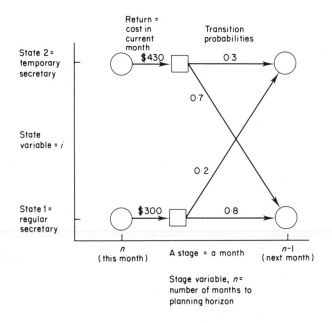

Figure 10.1 Hiring a secretary: formulation

regular secretary (state 1) next month is 0·8 and the probability of having a temporary (state 2) is 0·2. If there is a temporary (state 2) in the current month the cost is $430, the probability of having a regular secretary next month (state 1) is 0·7 and the probability of having a temporary (state 2) is 0·3. These states, returns, and transition probabilities are shown in Figure 10.1.

Let i be the state variable, so that $i = 1$ corresponds to having a regular secretary and $i = 2$ corresponds to having a temporary. If there are N states in all they are $i = 1, 2, \ldots, N$. The calculations are based on a finite number of stages and we let the stage variable n denote the number of months remaining in the planning period. Although the calculations are always carried out for a finite number of stages we shall see that we can deduce the steady-state solution from this.

Let $r(i)$ be the return or cost associated with a visit to state i. In our example $r(1) = \$300$ and $r(2) = \$430$. Let $p(i,j)$ be the probability that system goes to adjacent state j given that it is currently in state i. Thus, if $i = 1$ (regular secretary) and $j = 2$ (temporary) we have, from the problem data already given, $p(1, 2) = 0 \cdot 2$. This corresponds to the fact that, if we currently have a regular secretary, the probability of having a temporary next month (owing to the regular

Table 10.1   Hiring a secretary: data

| State | Cost | Transition probabilities | |
i	r(i)	p(i, 1)	p(1, 2)
1 = regular	300	0·8	0·2
2 = temporary	430	0·7	0·3

secretary resigning) is $0 \cdot 2$. This algebra and the problem data are summarized in Table 10·1.

Calculation Procedure for n Stages

The mean total cost of hiring a secretary over any given number of months can be calculated using the probabilistic decision network calculation procedure. This was described in Section 8.3, Chapter 8, and summarized algebraically in Section 8.5. In the current problem the calculations are simplified because no decisions are required. This is equivalent to having just one action per state.

Let $f(n, i)$ denote the mean total cost incurred when the system starts in state i and continues for n stages. This cost is the *value* of state i at stage n. The value of state i at stage n is given by the sum of the return $r(i)$ and the weighted values of the adjacent states. This weighted value, denoted w, is the sum of the values of the adjacent states multiplied by the probability of transition to each state. That is

$$f(n, i) = r(i) + \sum_{j=1}^{N} p(i,j) f(n-1, j) \tag{10.1}$$

or

$$f(n, i) = r(i) + w \tag{10.2}$$

where

$$w = \sum_{j=1}^{N} p(i,j) f(n-1, j) \tag{10.3}$$

This is summarized in Figure 10.2.

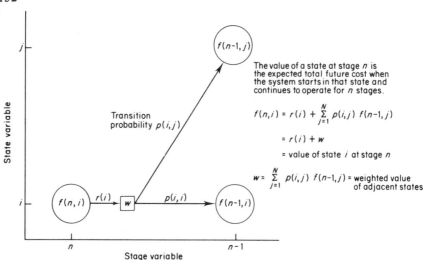

Figure 10.2   Markov process with returns: calculation procedure

Calculations for *n* Stages

In Figure 10.3 the mean costs have been calculated for a four month period. We shall show how the steady-state cost per month can be deduced from this, but first, we outline the calculations of Figure 10.3.

The calculations in Figure 10.3 start by giving the terminal states, that is the stage 0 or right-hand nodes, the value zero. The value of a state is the mean total future cost when the system starts in that state. At stage 1 the values of the adjacent states are all zero and so the weighted values are zero. The state values are simply equal to the returns and are 300 for state 1 and 430 for state 2.

At stage 2 consider state 1. There is a cost of 300 and then a probability 0·8 of transition to state 1 at stage 1, which has value 300 and probability 0·2 of transition to state 2 which has value 430. Hence the value of state 1 at stage 2 is given by

$$f(2, 1) = r(1) + \sum_{j=1}^{2} p(1,j)f(1,j)$$
$$= 300 + 0\cdot8 \times 300 + 0\cdot2 \times 430 \qquad (10.4)$$
$$= 626$$

Similarly the value of state 2 at stage 2 is given by

$$f(2, 2) = r(2) + \sum_{j=1}^{2} p(2,j)f(1,j)$$
$$= 430 + 0\cdot7 \times 300 + 0\cdot3 \times 430 \qquad (10.5)$$
$$= 769$$

Similar calculations yield the state values at stages 3 and 4 as shown in Figure 10.3.

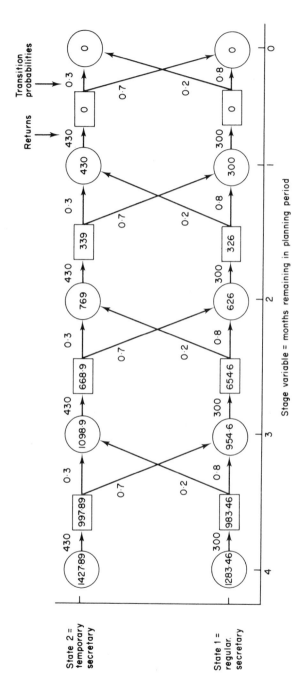

Figure 10.3　Hiring a secretary: expected costs over a four-month planning period

Value Differences and the Steady-State Gain

The steady-state average cost per month can be deduced by considering the differences in the values of the states from stage to stage. Let $d(n, i)$ be the value of state i at stage n minus the value of state i at stage $n - 1$, that is

$$d(n, i) = f(n, i) - f(n - 1, i), \quad n \geqslant 1 \qquad (10.6)$$

The value difference $d(n, i)$ is the mean total cost when the system starts in state i and continues for n months minus the mean total cost when the system starts in state i and

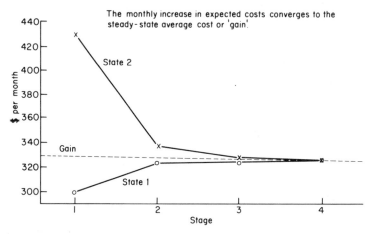

Figure 10.4   Hiring a secretary: monthly increase in expected costs (value differences in Table 10.2)

continues for $n - 1$ months. In other words it is the mean increase in costs when the planning period is extended by one month.

The behaviour of the value differences in the hiring a secretary example is shown in Table 10.2 and Figure 10.4. The value differences are converging to a value of about $328.9.

Table 10.2   *Hiring a secretary: state values and value differences*

Stage n	State i	Value $f(n, i)$	Value difference $d(n, i) = f(n, i) - f(n - 1, i)$
0	1	0	
0	2	0	
1	1	300	300
1	2	430	430
2	1	626	326
2	2	769	339
3	1	954·6	328·6
3	2	1098·9	329·9
4	1	1283·46	328·86
4	2	1427·89	328·99

As n increases, the value differences approach a common value which is called the steady-state gain and denoted by g, that is

$$d(n, i) \rightarrow g, \quad \text{the steady-state gain} \qquad (10.7)$$

Special Cases

There are two special cases where the value differences do not converge to the steady-state gain. The first of these is where the system consists of two or more completely independent subsystems. This is called a *multichain* system as opposed to the usual *unichain* system. In a multichain system each subsystem converges individually, but because the subsystems are independent, convergence to a single overall gain does not occur. The second case is a *periodic* system. This involves a form of regular movement round the states. In the hiring a secretary problem this corresponds to a situation where the employer had a regular secretary and a temporary in alternate months. On average this two-state system would spend half the time in each state, so that the average cost per month would be the average of the monthly costs of a regular and a temporary secretary. That is

$$(300 + 430)/2 = \$365 \text{ per month}$$

Systems which are not periodic are said to be aperiodic. Periodic systems can be converted into aperiodic form by applying the Schweitzer transformation (Chapter 13, Section 13.1) with $t(i, k) = 2$. The systems discussed in the remainder of this book are assumed to be unichain and aperiodic.

10.3 A Markov Decision Process

In a Markov decision process there is a system with states labelled $i = 1, \ldots, N$. In state i there are a number of actions available. If action k is chosen a return $r(i, k)$ is generated and the system goes to state j with probability $p(i, j, k), j = 1, \ldots, N$. A set of actions, one for each state, constitutes a *policy*. Under a given policy δ the system is a Markov process with returns and has steady-state gain $g(\delta)$. A policy which has the highest gain (or the lowest in a minimization problem) is an optimal policy δ^*, and its gain is the optimal gain, denoted g^*.

A policy whose gain differs from the optimum by not more than a known amount (usually small) is called a *tolerance optimal policy*. We illustrate the formulation and solution of Markov decision problems by adding a decision structure to the hiring a secretary example.

Hiring a secretary: decision problem

A man employs a secretary who may resign at the end of any month. The probability that a secretary will resign in the current month depends on the salary paid to him/her. When a secretary leaves a temporary is employed on a monthly contract, and the man attempts to find another regular secretary. The probability that he finds one in any month depends on the amount spent on advertising. For given cost and probability data we wish to find a policy (that is a combination of salary level and advertising expenditure) which minimizes the average cost per month.

For simplicity we consider only two levels of salary and two levels of advertising expenditure. The monthly costs and transition probabilities are shown in

Table 10.3   Hiring a secretary decision problem: data

State i	Action k	Cost (\$) $r(i, k)$	Transition probabilities	
			$p(i, 1, k)$	$p(i, 2, k)$
1 = regular secretary	1 = low salary	230	0·6	0·4
	2 = high salary	300	0·8	0·2
2 = temporary secretary	1 = cheap advertising	430	0·7	0·3
	2 = expensive advertising	460	0·9	0·1

Table 10.3. The problem is to find a tolerance optimal policy whose average monthly cost is minimal to an accuracy of, say, \$1 per month.

Formulation

State $i = 1$ corresponds to having a regular secretary and state $i = 2$ to having a temporary. In state 1 (regular), action $k = 1$ corresponds to paying a low salary, cost \$230 per month, and action $k = 2$ is to paying a high salary, cost \$300 per month. In state 2 (temporary), action $k = 1$ corresponds to using cheap advertising, giving an associated cost of \$430, and action $k = 2$ to expensive advertising, giving an associated cost of \$460. The cost in the current month given that the system is in state i and that action k is used is $r(i, k)$, and the transition probabilities are $p(i, j, k)$ as shown in Table 10.3. The formulation is summarized in Figure 10.5.

Four different policies are possible, namely:

(a) low salary, cheap advertising;
(b) low salary, expensive advertising;
(c) high salary, cheap advertising;
(d) high salary, expensive advertising.

Each policy has a corresponding steady-state average cost per month and the aim is to find the cheapest, to within a reasonable tolerance. Policy (c) is the same as was considered in Section 10.2 and we know that the steady-state cost is \$329 per month. A possible method would be to evaluate each policy in the manner of Section 10.2, however, in a larger problem which might have thousands of policies such an approach would be impractical. The method we use is to apply the usual decision network calculation procedure for a number of stages. As the calculation proceeds we use the value differences to enable us to decide when a tolerance op-

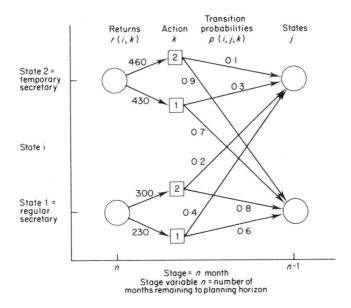

Figure 10.5   Hiring a secretary decision problem: formulation

timal policy has been found. An additional feature of the calculation procedure is a test which can identify some actions as non-optimal at the current stage without the necessity for determining the precise value of those actions.

10.4 The Action Elimination Algorithm

The minimal expected total cost of hiring a secretary over any given number of months can be calculated using the probabilistic decision network procedure described in Chapter 8, Section 8.3. The data are now the same at each stage. The bounds, convergence test, and action elimination test which are used to give an efficient determination of a tolerance optimal policy are described in this section. The whole procedure is called the action elimination algorithm after the key action elimination test which it incorporates. A flow chart for the procedure is in Figure 10.6 and a numerical example is the next section.

Let $f(n, i)$ denote the minimum mean total return generated in a process which starts in state i and continues for n stages; this quantity is the *value* of state i at stage n. The terminal values can be arbitrarily chosen. State values for stages $n = 1,2,3 \ldots$ are computed using the dynamic programming recurrence relation:

$$f(n, i) = \underset{k}{\text{Min}} \left(r(i, k) + \sum_{i=1}^{v} p(i, j, k) f(n-1, j) \right) \tag{10.8}$$

Our aim is to find a policy with minimal long-term average costs and as in Section

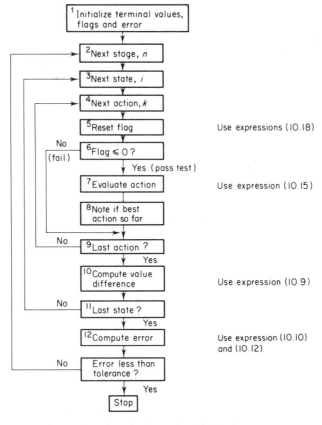

Figure 10.6   Flow chart for the action elimination algorithm: the 'flag' for each action is the action elimination test quantity, $z(n, i, k)$

10.2, we consider the increase in the value of state i from stage to stage. Let $d(n, i)$ be the value state i at stage n minus the value of stage i at state $n - 1$, that is

$$d(n, i) = f(n, i) - f(n - 1, i) \qquad (10.9)$$

The value difference is the increase in the minimum mean total costs when the planning period is extended from $n - 1$ months to n months. Schweitzer (1965) shows that, provided the system is aperiodic under all policies, the value differences $d(n, i)$, $i = 1, \ldots, N$, converge as n increases to a quantity g^* which is the gain of the system under an optimal policy. In our example g^* is the minimum long-term average cost per month.

Bounds and Convergence Test

The convergence of the value differences is monitored as follows. Let $d_U(n)$ be the largest and $d_L(n)$ the smallest value difference at stage n, that is

$$d_U(n) = \operatorname*{Max}_i[d(n, i)], \quad d_L(n) = \operatorname*{Min}_i[d(n, i)] \qquad (10.10)$$

Let δ_n be the optimizing policy found at stage n by application of equation (10.8). That is, δ_n is the set of optimizing actions, one for each state, which is selected for use at the current stage when the planning horizon is n stages away. This policy has a steady-state gain or cost which we denote $g(\delta_n)$ which is currently unknown. From the results of Odoni (1969) and Hastings (1971) the following bounds apply at stage n:

$$d_L(n-1) \leqslant d(n, i) \leqslant d_U(n-1)$$

$$d_L(n) \leqslant g(\delta_n) \leqslant g^* \, d_U(n) \quad \text{if maximizing} \tag{10.11}$$

$$d_L(n) \leqslant g^* \, g(\delta_n) \leqslant d_U(n) \quad \text{if minimizing}$$

Let the *error* at stage n be $e(n)$ defined by

$$e(n) = d_U(n) - d_L(n) \tag{10.12}$$

Equations (10.11) and (10.12) imply that

$$|g^* - g(\delta_n)| \leqslant e(n) \tag{10.13}$$

Also let the *approximate gain* be $\hat{g}(n)$ defined by

$$\hat{g}(n) = \tfrac{1}{2}[d_U(n) + d_L(n)] \tag{10.14}$$

Hence the following results apply at stage n:

(1) The current policy is tolerance optimal if the error $e(n)$ is less than the prescribed tolerance.
(2) The gain of the system under the tolerance optimal policy is $\hat{g}(n) \pm \tfrac{1}{2}e(n)$.

These results enable us to monitor the convergence of the algorithm and to discontinue the calculation as soon as a tolerance optimal policy and its approximate gain have been determined within any prescribed accuracy.

Action Elimination

Let the quantity in large parentheses on the right-hand side of equation (10.8) be called the value of action k at state i and stage n. This will be denoted $f(n, i, k)$ so that,

$$f(n, i, k) = r(i, k) + \sum_{i=1}^{N} p(i, j, k) f(n-1, j) \tag{10.15}$$

The quantity just defined is the mean cost over n stages when the system starts in state i, action k is taken immediately and optimal actions are taken thereafter.

The absolute difference between the optimal value of a state and the value of action k at that state is called the *shortfall* of action k and is denoted $y(n, i, k)$. That is

$$y(n, i, k) = |f(n, i) - f(n, i, k)| \tag{10.16}$$

The absolute difference is used in defining the shortfall so that it applies equally to maximization and minimization problems. The shortfall of an action is the reduction in expected total return (or increase in costs) when that action is used at the current state instead of the optimal action.

Hastings (1976) shows that the shortfall of an action at stage $n + 1$ cannot be less than the shortfall at stage n minus the error at stage n, that is

$$y(n + 1, i, k) \geqslant y(n, i, k) - e(n) \qquad (10.17)$$

It follows that if the shortfall $y(n, i, k)$ exceeds the error $e(n)$ then action k cannot be the action which maximizes the value of state i at stage $n + 1$. Furthermore, if

$$y(n, i, k) > e(n) + e(n + 1)$$

action k cannot be optimal at stage $n + 2$ and so on.

Thus we can define a test quantity $z(n, i, k)$, called the action elimination test quantity, as follows:

$$z(1, i, k) = 0$$

$$z(n, i, k) = \begin{cases} y(n-1, i, k) - e(n-1) & \text{if } z(n-1, i, k) \leqslant 0 \\ z(n-1, i, k) - e(n-1) & \text{if } z(n-1, i, k) > 0 \end{cases} \qquad (10.18)$$

for $n = 2, 3, 4, \ldots$.

Actions for which $z(n, i, k) > 0$ are said to 'fail the test' at stage n. For these actions the time consuming step of evaluating the right-hand side of equation (10.15) is avoided. Actions may fail the test for a few stages and then pass it again, but as convergence proceeds the error decreases and we soon find that the proportion of actions which pass the test become small. At least one action in each state will always pass the test since there must be an optimizing action.

A flow chart of the algorithm is shown in Figure 10.6.

10.5 Calculations

The calculations involved in determining a tolerance optimal policy for the hiring a secretary decision problem are shown in Table 10.4. These calculations are now described with the aid of the flow chart. The optimal state values $f(n, i)$ are also shown plotted against stage number, n, in Figure 10.7.

The terminal values $f(0, i)$ can be chosen arbitrarily and we shall set them to zero. For the sake of brevity, the action elimination test quantities are referred to as the flags. The flags are initially set zero. An action fails the test whenever its flag is positive.

Stage 1

At stage 1 the flags are zero and all actions are evaluated. With zero terminal values the value of an action is simply the cost in the current month. In state 1

Table 10.4 Solution of the hiring a secretary decision problem by the action elimination algorithm

Stage n	State i	Action k	Flag z(n,i,k)	Value of action, f(n,i,k) * = optimal value f(n,i)	Shortfall y(n,i,k)	Value difference d(n,i) U = upper bound L = lower bound		Error e(n)
1	1 =regular secretary	1 = low salary	0	230*	0	230	L	
		2 = high salary	0	300	70			200
	2 = temporary secretary	1 = cheap ads	0	430*	0	430	U	
		2 = expensive ads	0	460	30			
2	1	1	−200	230 + 0·6 × 230 + 0·4 × 430 = 540*	0	310	U	
		2	−130	300 + 0·8 × 230 + 0·2 × 430 = 570	30			30
	2	1	−200	430 + 0·7 × 230 + 0·3 × 430 = 720	10	280	L	
		2	−170	460 + 0·9 × 230 + 0·1 × 430 = 710*	0			
3	1	1	−30	230 + 0·6 × 540 + 0·4 × 710 = 838*	0	298	L	
		2	0	300 + 0·8 × 540 + 0·2 × 710 = 874	36			9
	2	1	−20	430 + 0·7 × 540 + 0·3 × 710 = 1021	4	307	U	
		2	−30	460 + 0·9 × 540 + 0·1 × 710 = 1017*	0			
4	1	1	−9	230 + 0·6 × 838 + 0·4 × 1017 = 1139·6*	0	301·6	U	
		2	27	non-optimal				2·7
	2	1	−5	430 + 0·7 × 838 + 0·3 × 1017 = 1321·7	5·8	298·9	L	
		2	−9	460 + 0·9 × 838 + 0·1 × 1017 = 1315·9*	0			
5	1	1	−2·7	230 + 0·6 × 1139·6 + 0·4 × 1315·9 = 1440·12*	0	300·52	L	
		2	24·3	non-optimal				0·81
	2	1	3·1	non-optimal		301·33	U	
		2	−2·7	460 + 0·9 × 1139·6 + 0·1 × 1315·9 = 1617·23*	0			

Tolerance optimal policy = low salary, expensive advertising; steady-state average monthly cost $300.93 ± 0.41 ≈ $301.

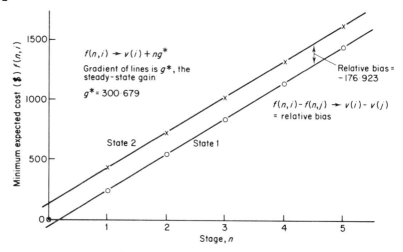

Figure 10.7   State values in the hiring of a secretary decision problem from Table 10.4 illustrating the gain and relative bias values from Table 10.7

these costs are \$230 for action 1 (low salary) and \$300 for action 2 (high salary). Action 1 is cheaper and is therefore optimal, giving $f(1, 1) = 230$. The shortfall of action 2 is $y(1, 1, 2) = |230 - 300| = 70$. The shortfall of the optimizing action is necessarily zero. The value difference for state 1 is $d(1, 1) = 230 - 0 = 230$.

In state 2 the costs are \$430 for action 1 (cheap advertising) and \$460 for action 2 (expensive advertising). Action 1 is optimal and the value of state 2 is $f(1, 2) = 430$. The shortfall of action 2 is $y(1, 1, 2) = |430 - 460| = 30$. The value difference for state 2 is $d(1, 2) = 430 - 0 = 430$.

The largest value difference at stage 1 is \$430 and the smallest is \$230. The policy identified at stage 1 is to use action 1 in each state, and this is policy δ_1. Inequalities (10.11) apply, that is,

$$230 \leqslant g^* \leqslant g(\delta_1) \leqslant 430$$

The error $e(1) = 430 - 230 = 200$. This concludes the calculations at stage 1.

Stage 2

At stage 2 and subsequently the first step in processing each action is to re-set the action elimination test quantity or flag (flow chart box 5). The value to which the flag is re-set depends on whether the action passed the test at the previous stage. If it did the flag becomes equal to the shortfall minus the error, otherwise it becomes equal to its previous value minus the error (see expressions (10.18)).

We next test the updated flag (flow chart box 6). If it is positive the action fails the test and is eliminated from further consideration at this stage; we then pass on to the next action (flow chart box 4). If the flag is non-positive (that is, negative or zero) the action passes the test and may be optimal at this stage; we then evaluate the action (flow chart box 7). This is the most time consuming step in the calculation. The value of the action is compared with the best value so far and the best action and value noted, so that when all actions have been processed the optimal action and the optimal value of the state, $f(n, i)$, will have been determined.

For state 1 action 1 the flag becomes $z(2, 1, 1) = y(1, 1, 1) - e(1) = 0 - 200 = -200$. The updated flag is negative so the action passes the test, and is evaluated giving

$$f(2, 1, 1) = r(1, 1) + \sum_{j=1}^{2} p(1, j, 1) f(1, j)$$
$$= 230 + 0 \cdot 6 \times 230 + 0 \cdot 4 \times 430 = 540$$

For state 1, action 2, the flag becomes $z(2, 1, 2) = y(1, 1, 2) - e(1) = 70 - 200 = -130$. The updated flag is again negative so this action also passes the test, and is evaluated giving

$$f(2, 1, 2) = r(1, 2) + \sum_{j=1}^{2} p(1, j, 2) f(1, j)$$
$$= 300 + 0 \cdot 8 \times 230 + 0 \cdot 2 \times 430 = 570$$

Action 1 gives the lower expected cost of \$540 and is therefore optimal at state 1, stage 2. We have now completed the action loop and can compute the value difference (flow chart box 10). This is $f(2, 1) - f(1, 1) = 540 - 230 = 310$.

A similar sequence of steps applies for state 2. No actions are eliminated. The values of actions 1 and 2 are \$720 and \$710 respectively and action 2 is optimal, giving $f(2, 2) = 710$. The value difference for state 2 is $f2, 2) - f(1, 2) = 710 - 430 = 280$. Thus the largest and smallest value differences are respectively \$310 and \$280, and the error is $e(2) = 310 - 280 = 30$. The policy identified at stage 2 is action 1 in state 1 and action 2 in state 2, and this is policy δ_2. Applying inequalities (10.11) and (10.13), we have

$$280 \leqslant g^* \leqslant g(\delta_2) \leqslant 310$$
$$g(\delta_2) - g^* \leqslant 30$$

Stage 3

Stage 3 is similar in principle to stage 2 and again no actions are eliminated, although the flag just reaches the value zero for action 2 in state 1. The calculations are shown in Table 10.4. The policy δ_3 is the same as δ_2 and the bounds narrow down to \$298 and \$307 giving an error of \$9.

Stage 4

At stage 4 we start as usual with state 1, action 1, which again passes the test.

This action was optimal for state 1 at stage 3, and we can see that an action which is optimal at stage $n - 1$ will always pass the test at stage n, since its shortfall is necessarily zero. The value action 1 is calculated, giving \$1139.6.

Action 2 at state 1 is now considered. This action passed the test at stage 3 where it had a shortfall of 36. The updated flag is therefore $z(4, 1, 2) = y(3, 1, 2) - e(3) = 36 - 9 = 27$. The flag is positive so the action fails the test and need not be evaluated. This is the first action to fail the test. Since there are no more actions at state 1, action 1 must be optimal and the state value is $f(4, 1) = 1139.6$.

At state 2 both actions pass the test. The policy δ_4 is again the same as δ_2 and the bounds narrow down to \$298.9 and \$301.6 giving an error of \$2.7.

Stage 5

At state 1, action 1 again passes the test and is evaluated. Action 2 failed the test at stage 4 so its updated flag is given by $z(5, 1, 2) = z(4, 1, 2) - e$ $(4) = 27 - 2 \cdot 7 = 24 \cdot 3$. The updated flag is positive and action 2 fails the test again.

At state 2, action 1 passed the test at stage 4, where its shortfall was $5 \cdot 8$. Its updated flag is $z(5, 2, 1) = y(4, 2, 1) - e(4) = 5 \cdot 8 - 2 \cdot 7 = 3 \cdot 1$. This is positive so the action fails the test and is not evaluated. Action 2 passes the test and has value \$1617·23. The policy δ_5 is again low salary and expensive advertising. The upper and lower bounds are 301.33 and 300.52 and the error is 0.81.

The error is now less than \$1 and is therefore within tolerance. Policy δ_5 is tolerance optimal, since its gain differs from the optimum by not more than the error of 81 cents. Inequalities (10.11) and (10.13) now give

$$300 \cdot 52 \leqslant g^* \leqslant g(\delta_5) \leqslant 301 \cdot 33$$
$$g(\delta_5) - g^* \leqslant 0 \cdot 81$$

Conclusion

The calculations shown in Table 10.4 yield the result that, to an accuracy of better than \$1 per month, the policy of low salary and expensive advertising gives the minimal steady-state average cost, and that this cost is \$301 per month.

10.6 Further Computational Methods

Other Algorithms

Many algorithms have been developed for solving Markov decision problems. An early and elegant technique was the policy iteration algorithm of Howard (1960). Linear programming has also been used and the formulations are summarized by Mine and Osaki (1970). The development of bounding procedures and the action elimination test has, however, made the algorithm presented in the last section the most efficient computationally and it is also the least demanding in computer core storage. It is particularly well suited to large-scale problems (Su and Deininger 1972).

Dynacode

Markov decision problems can be solved using Dynacode. The input for the hiring a secretary decision problem is shown in Table 10.5 and the output in Table 10.6.

Table 10.5   Hiring a secretary decision problem: Dynacode input

```
DYNACODE HIRING A SECKETARY
LIST INPUT
MINIMISE
STOCHASTIC
TERMINAL STATES 2
ZERO TERMINAL VALUES
RANK 2
INFINITE STAGE
STAGES 100
TOLERANCE 0.001
* STATE 1 IS REGULAR SECRETARY FOR WHICH:
            * ACTION 1 IS LOW SALARY
            * ACTION 2 IS HIGH SALARY
* STATE 2 IS TEMPORARY SECRETARY FOR WHICH:
            * ACTION 1 IS CHEAP ADVERTISING
            * ACTION 2 IS EXPENSIVE ADVERTISING
DATA
1,1,1,230,0
1,1,1,0.6,1
1,1,1,0.4,2
1,1,2,300,0
1,1,2,0.8,1
1,1,2,0.2,2
1,2,1,430,0
1,2,1,0.7,1
1,2,1,0.3,2
1,2,2,460,0
1,2,2,0.9,1
1,2,2,0.1,2
END
```

The statement INFINITE STAGE is used to indicate that a steady-state solution to a long-term problem is required. Dynacode uses the dynamic programming algorithm and checks for convergence by using the bounds and error indicated in inequalities (10.11) and (10.13). The user specifies a tolerance using the statement TOLERANCE y where y is a positive real number. Computation is discontinued when the error becomes less than y and the resulting tolerance optimal policy is printed. In Table 10.5 a tolerance of 0·001 is specified. The user also uses the statement STAGES n which now specifies the maximum number of stages or iterations to be computed. If convergence within tolerance does not occur within the specified number of stages, computation stops at stage n and the policy found at that stage is printed. The terminal values may be entered as data, or, as in Table 10.5, set to zero using the statement ZERO TERMINAL VALUES. The data must be stationary and are entered as data for stage 1, in the stochastic format described in the summary of Dynacode in Chapter 14. As well as determining a tolerance optimal policy, Dynacode can be used to rank the actions, and in Table 10.5 RANK 2 has been specified.

The Dynacode output, Table 10.6, contains a table headed BEST ACTION LIST TO RANK 2 and a table headed TOLERANCE OPTIMAL POLICY. In

Table 10.6   Hiring a secretary decision problem: Dynacode output

```
DYNACODE HIRING A SECRETARY
* STATE 1 IS REGULAR SECRETARY FOR WHICH:
          * ACTION 1 IS LOW SALARY
          * ACTION 2 IS HIGH SALARY
* STATE 2 IS TEMPORARY SECRETARY FOR WHICH:
          * ACTION 1 IS CHEAP ADVERTISING
          * ACTION 2 IS EXPENSIVE ADVERTISING
*
BEST ACTION LIST TO RANK     2
*
          STAGE          STATE          ACTION          VALUE
           12              1              1             300.769
           12              1              2             335.384
           12              2              2             300.769
           12              2              1             306.153
*
TOLERANCE OPTIMAL POLICY
*
          STAGE          STATE          ACTION          VALUE
           12              1              1            -176.923
           12              2              2               0.000
*
          GAIN        LOWER BOUND      UPPER BOUND
         300.769        300.769          300.769
END
```

the latter table the STAGE column gives the number of stages required for convergence or the stage limit if this is less. In the example, convergence to within tolerance occurs at stage 15. The STATE and ACTION columns indicate the policy found, which in this case is action 1 in state 1 and action 2 in state 2, i.e., low salary and expensive advertising as found in the hand calculations of Section 10.5. Below the policy table, the gain and the lower and upper bounds on the gain are given. The figure given for the gain is the average of the upper and lower bounds, that is the approximate gain $\hat{g}(n)$ defined by equation (10.14). The gain of the tolerance optimal policy is \$300.769, which lies within the tolerance band found in Table 10.4.

Relative Bias Values

The entries in the VALUE column of the TOLERANCE OPTIMAL POLICY table in Table 10.6 give the state values $f(n, i)$ at stage 15, relative to the value of state N at that stage. For state i the entry is $f(n, i) - f(n, N)$. These quantities are called the relative bias values of the states and can provide useful cost information. In the example state 1 has a relative bias value of $-\$176.92$. This means that a process which starts in state 1 (regular secretary) will have a cost advantage of $\$176.92$ relative to a process which starts in state 2 (temporary secretary). The long run average cost per month is the same regardless of which state the system starts in, but there is a finite cost advantage in starting in a favourable state.

A graphical interpretation of the relative bias values is shown in Figure 10.7. As n increases, the state value $f(n, i)$ has the form

$$f(n, i) \rightarrow v(i) + ng^* \tag{10.19}$$

where g^* is the optimal gain. It follows that

$$f(n, i) - f(n, j) \rightarrow v(i) - v(j) \tag{10.20}$$

where $v(i) - v(j)$ is the bias of state i relative to state j. Figure 10.7 shows the state values $f(n, i)$, which were calculated in Table 10.4, plotted against stage number, n. As convergence proceeds the value differences approach the steady-state optimal gain g^*, so that the state values are asymptotic to lines of gradient $g^* = 300.769$.

The values of the states are asymptotic to parallel lines whose vertical separation corresponds to the relative bias of the states. From Table 10.4 we have $f(5, 12) - f(5, 2) = 1440 \cdot 12 - 1617 \cdot 23 = -177 \cdot 11$. This is close to the relative bias value $-176 \cdot 923$ computed by Dynacode (Table 10.7). The practical interpretation of this is that if we are about to start a month with a temporary secretary it would be worth paying up to $\$176.92$ to acquire a regular secretary instantly.

The relative bias values satisfy the equation (assuming maximization):

$$v(i) + g^* = \underset{k}{\text{Max}}\left(r(i, k) + \sum_{j=1}^{N} p(i, j, k) v(j) \right) \tag{10.21}$$

Hence, if the state values are equal to the relative bias values a further iteration will increase all the state values by g^*. This will leave the relative bias values unchanged, so that we have reached the fixed point to which the dynamic programming algorithm converges.

Ranking the Actions

The shortfall of an action is a measure of how close it is to optimality at any given stage. It therefore forms a basis for ranking the actions. We define a quantity called the *action difference* which leads to bounds on the gain for all policies. The action difference for stage n, state i, action k is denoted $d(n, i, k)$ and defined by

$$d(n, i, k) = f(n, i, k) - f(n-1, i) \tag{10.22}$$

The action difference is related to the state value difference and the shortfall by the equations

$$d(n, i, k) = f(n, k) - f(n - 1, i) - [f(n, i) - f(n, i, k)] \qquad (10.23a)$$

$$= \begin{cases} d(n, i) - y(n, i, k) & \text{if maximizing} \qquad (10.23b) \\ d(n, i) + y(n, i, k) & \text{if minimizing} \qquad (10.23c) \end{cases}$$

To illustrate the action differences by a numerical example we consider the results obtained at stage 3 of the hiring a secretary decision problem, as derived in Table 10.4. As this is a minimization problem, the action differences are given by the sum of the state value difference and the shortfall. The ranks and action differences are summarized in Table 10.7.

Table 10.7   Action differences and ranks for stage 3 of the hiring a secretary decision problem

State i	Value difference $d(3, i)$	Action k	Shortfall $y(3, i, k)$	Action difference $d(3, i, k)$	Rank
1	298	1	0	298	1
1	298	2	36	334	2
2	307	1	4	311	2
2	307	2	0	307	1

In each state the action with the smallest shortfall has rank 1, the action with second smallest shortfall has rank 2 and so on.

Bounds on the Gain of Any Policy

For any policy δ, the action differences are value differences for that policy. The largest and smallest action differences are respectively upper and lower bounds on the gain of the policy. From Table 10.7 we see, for example, that the policy of taking action 1 in each state has a lower bound of 298 and an upper bound of 311. The action differences give bounds on the gain of any policy.

10.7 Policy Constraints

The methods discussed so far relate to problems where policies can be formed from any combination of actions. In some practical situations only certain combinations of actions are permitted and the problem is then said to have policy constraints. For example, in the hiring a secretary problem the combination of low salary with expensive advertising might be inadmissible.

If the policy constraints are such that only a few policies are allowed, we can find the best simply by evaluating the gain of each permitted policy. If there are a large number of permitted policies the following procedure can be used.

We first apply the action elimination algorithm to the problem without policy constraints. We then use the action differences to list the policies in sequence of increasing lower bound. Policies with the same lower bound are listed in sequence of increasing upper bound. (In maximization problems the sequence is reversed.) The listing derived from Table 10.7 is shown in Table 10.8.

Suppose that every policy is feasible except policy 1 in Table 10.8, and that we wish to find a tolerance optimal policy with this constraint. Let the tolerance be $3.50, that is, we wish to find a policy whose gain is within $3.50 of the minimum. The method of solution is as follows. We work down the feasible policy list in the sequence of Table 10.8 and consider the policies one at a time. At any point we have a current best policy B and the next policy on the list, policy C. If we reach a policy C and find that its lower bound, denoted C_L, plus the tolerance t is greater than or equal to the upper bound of the best policy, denoted B_U, then policy B is optimal. Otherwise we apply value iteration to policy C and at each stage we check if the revised lower bound C_L plus the tolerance t is greater than the best

Table 10.8   Policies listed in sequence of lower and upper bound

	Actions		Bounds on gain	
Policy	state 1	state 2	lower	upper
1	1	2	298	307
2	1	1	298	311
3	2	2	307	334
4	2	1	311	334

upper bound B_U. If so we move on to the next policy. If not, we continue until the bounds C_L, C_L converge within tolerance. If $C_U < B_U$, C replaces B as the best policy so far. We then continue to the next policy on the list. In a large problem it may be necessary to stop before finding a tolerance optimal policy. However, we always know that the remaining error cannot exceed $B_U - C_L$, where C is the next policy on the list when the search stops. A flow chart for the method is given in Figure 10.8.

We shall apply the method to the policy list of Table 10.8, assuming that policy 1 is infeasible. Policy 2 is the first policy so at step 3 of Figure 10.8 we have $B_U = 311$. Policy 2 is now also the 'next policy', C. We move forward through step 5 to step 6 and apply value iteration. We always take the latest relative bias values as the terminal state values. From Table 10.5 the state values at stage 3 were $f(3, 1) = 838, f(3, 2) = 1017$ and so one stage of value iteration under policy 2 gives

$$f(4, 1, 1) = r(1, 1) + \sum_{j=1}^{2} p(1, j, 1) f(3, j)$$
$$= 230 + 0.6 \times 838 + 0.4 \times 1017 = 1139.6$$

$$f(4, 2, 1) = r(2, 1) + \sum_{j=1}^{2} p(2, j, 1) f(3, j)$$
$$= 430 + 0.7 \times 838 + 0.3 \times 1017 = 1321.7$$

B = best policy so far, C is next policy on list, t = tolerance

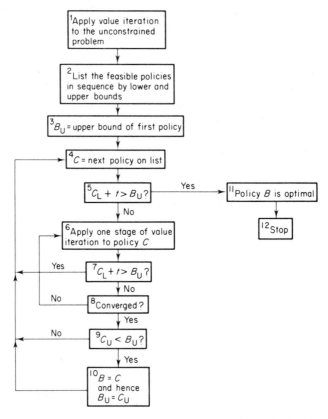

Figure 10.8   Policy constraints algorithm (minimization)

The action differences are calculated and we find that $C_L = 301 \cdot 6$, $C_U = 304 \cdot 7$. We move via steps 7 and 8 to step 9 of Figure 10.8 where we find that $C_U < B_U$ so the new upper bound becomes $B_U = 304 \cdot 7$. Returning to step 4, C becomes policy 3. Now at step 5 we find that $C_L + t = 307 + 3 \cdot 5 > B_U = 304 \cdot 7$. Hence policy B, that is policy 2, is tolerance optimal for the policy constrained problem.

CHAPTER 11

The Repair Limit Replacement Method

11.1 Equipment Replacement Strategies

All types of equipment require repair from time to time, and eventually replacement. Various strategies have been devised for making repair/replacement decisions in differing circumstances. The purpose of the present chapter is to describe the repair limit replacement method, which is applicable to large-scale replacement problems and can produce substantial savings over the widely used economic life method. The repair limit method is used to control vehicle replacement in the British Army (Hastings 1970, Mahon and Bailey 1975). Repair limit decision problems can be formulated and solved as Markov decision problems, using the principles developed in Chapter 10. As a preliminary we consider the form of the economic life and repair limit replacement methods.

Economic Life

In the economic life replacement method all repairs required by items of a given type are carried out until they reach a certain age at which time they are replaced. The replacement age is determined by a consideration of cost factors and is called the economic life. The economic life minimizes average costs per unit time within the context of the strategy of replacing all items at the same age. However, this is not the best form of replacement strategy.

In practice, repair costs arise in a probabilistic way. An item which is getting near to the replacement age may need an expensive repair, which, under a pure economic life policy would have to be carried out. The policy therefore tends to be modified, at least in extreme cases. For example, a vehicle which is involved in a road accident may be written off instead of being repaired.

Repair Limits

The repair limit replacement method eliminates high cost repairs but takes advantage of items which survive with only cheap repairs. Replacement is only considered when a repair is required. At that point the cost of the required repair is estimated and is compared with a quantity called the 'repair limit'. If the estimated repair cost is less than the repair limit the item is repaired, otherwise it is replaced. The value of the repair limit depends on the type and age of the item and may also vary with location and service conditions.

Repair limit strategies can be applied in a range of different situations. In the regular inspection problem items are inspected at regular intervals, for example, annually. The cost of repairs required to keep the item in service for a further year is estimated and compared with a repair limit. If the repair limit is exceeded the item is replaced, otherwise it continues in service for another year. Repair cost estimates may turn out to be incorrect, but the validity of the approach will not be affected provided that the estimates are unbiased.

In the 'random failure' model failures are assumed to occur in accordance with an age dependent failure rate. This is the model applied to Army vehicle replacements. The stage variable may be miles or hours run rather than age, or may be related to the condition of the item in a more general way. The use of repair limits is usually combined with an age limit. Items which reach the age limit are replaced regardless of repair costs. This is done to avoid retaining obsolescent items and their associated spare parts. This age limit may be different from the economic life. Re-sale can also be combined with a repair limit strategy.

Approximate repair limits can be determined by a rule of thumb which states that no more should be spent on the repair of an item than the item will be worth when it is repaired. The idea of 'worth' in this context is only meaningful if a market exists in which values are much the same for other people as for the decision maker. This is true for the individual car owner in relation to the secondhand car market, but otherwise may well not apply. A second method of approximation is to apply declining balance (exponential) depreciation over the estimated useful life of the items.

The more exact method of calculating repair limits is by formulating the replacement problem as a Markov decision problem, and this technique is now described with the aid of an example.

11.2 Regular Inspection Problem

Vehicles of a certain type are inspected annually and an estimate is made of the cost of repairs required to keep each vehicle in service for a further year.

A repair limit replacement strategy is applied, so that a replacement is made if the repair cost exceeds a repair limit. Otherwise the vehicle is repaired as necessary and retained until the next inspection, when a further decision is made. Vehicles which reach a certain age limit are always replaced.

The vehicles in question are heavily utilized and have an age limit of three years. The cost of a new vehicle is $15,000. In the first year of life no costs are incurred because the vehicles are under warranty. At the end of the first year of life the vehicles are inspected and an estimate is made of the cost of keeping each vehicle in service for a further year. This estimated cost varies from vehicle to vehicle. An analysis of inspection records shows these costs have a negative exponential distribution with mean $5000. Under a negative exponential distribution with mean m, the probability density for the value x is $f(x) = (1/m) \exp(=x/m)$ (see Figure 11.3). A repair limit is applied to these costs and vehicles for which the estimated exceeds the repair limit are replaced. The remaining vehicles are repaired as required and proceed until they reach age 2 years. A similar procedure then applies, but the mean estimated cost at age 2 is $7500. We wish to determine optimal repair limits which minimize the steady-state average cost per vehicle per year of repairs plus replacements.

Formulation

The problem is formulated as shown in Figures 11.1 and 11.2. The state variable, i, is the age of a vehicle. A stage is a year. The action variable, k, is the repair limit. In principle the repair limit is a continuous variable, but it is sufficient in practice to consider a few discrete values. The return $r(i, k)$ is the mean total cost of repairs plus replacements at age i given repair limit k. The transition probabilities are the probability of replacement $p(i, 1, k)$ and the probability of repair $p(i, i + 1, k)$.

Data Calculations

Formulae for the expected total cost in the current year and for the probabilities of repair and replacement are derived in Section 11.3. The results relevant to the current problem are as follows. For vehicles of age i with mean estimated repair cost m, repair limit k, and replacement cost A the probabilities of replacement and repair are respectively:

$$\text{probability of replacement} = \exp(-k/m) = P \qquad (11.1)$$

$$\text{probability of repair} = -\exp(-k/m) = 1 - P \qquad (11.2)$$

and the mean total cost of repairs plus replacements per vehicle is

$$\text{cost} = m[1 - P(1 + k/m)] + AP \qquad (11.3)$$

Equations (11.1) to (11.3) enable us to calculate the returns and transitions probabilities corresponding to any given values of the mean estimated repair cost, repair limit, and acquisition cost. A first approximation to the optimum repair limits can be made by estimating the depreciated value of the item at the time of inspection. A simple linear depreciation of a new item costing $15,000 and having a three-year life gives depreciated values of $10,000 at age 1 and $5000 at age 2. To seek out the optimum repair limit policy we add a range of alternative repair limit values in the region of our initial estimates. We then calculate the returns and transition probabilities for each state (age) and action (repair limit value) using equations (11.1) to (11.3).

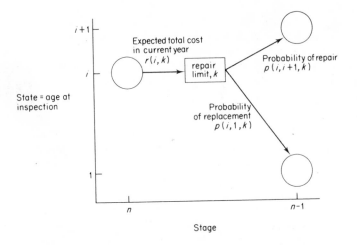

Figure 11.1   Repair limit decision network: basic components

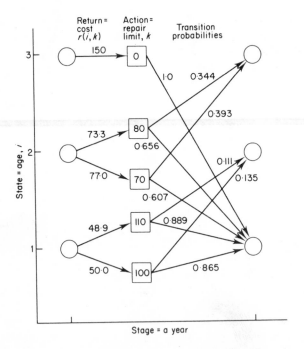

Figure 11.2   Regular inspection repair limit problem: the
decision network ($100 units)

The following range of repair limit values has been selected for the current problem:

Age 1   Repair limits $10,000, 11,000, 12,000, 13,000
Age 2   Repair limits $5000, 6000, 7000, 8000, 9000, 10,000

After we have optimized over a given set of repair limits it may become clear that we need to vary the range of alternative repair limit values and then carry out a further optimization. The steady-state average cost is not sensitive to small changes in the repair limits and it is not necessary to achieve great precision in determining the repair limit values.

The labour of hand calculation of returns and transition probabilities can be avoided by writing a small computer program which reads the acquisition cost, mean estimated repair cost, and a range of repair limit values, and calculates and prints the expected total cost of repairs and replacements, the probability of replacement and the probability of repair. Table 11.1(a) shows such a program written in BASIC and Table 11.1(b) shows the output when the program is run. Different results can be obtained by varying the data. Results obtained for the range of costs and repair limits

Table 11.1(a)   BASIC program for repair limit data calculations: regular inspection problem

```
10    REMARK REPAIR LIMIT REGULAR INSPECTION DATA CALCULATIONS
20    READ A
30    PRINT "ACQUISITION COST"A
40    READ M
50    PRINT "MEAN REPAIR COST"M
60    PRINT
70    READ N
80    PRINT "REPAIR LIMIT","TOTAL COST","PROB. REPLACE","PROB. REPAIR"
90    FOR I=1 TO N
100   READ K
110   P=EXP(-K/M)
120   C=M*(1-P*(1+K/M))
130   R=C+A*P
140   PRINT K,R,P,1-P
150   NEXT I
160   REMARK ACQUISITION COST
170   DATA 150
180   REMARK MEAN ESTIMATED REPAIR COST
190   DATA 75
200   REMARK NO. OF REPAIR LIMITS, REPAIR LIMITS,...
210   DATA 5,50,60,70,80,90
220   END
```

Table 11.1(b)   Results from running the program shown in Table 11.1(a)

ACQUISITION COST 150
MEAN REPAIR COST 75

REPAIR LIMIT	TOTAL COST	PROB. REPLACE	PROB. REPAIR
50	87.8354	.513417	.486583
60	81.7399	.449329	.550671
70	76.9662	.393241	.606759
80	73.2792	.344154	.655846
90	70.4821	.301194	.698806

used in the current problem are summarized in Table 11.2. All costs and repair limits shown in the tables are expressed in hundred dollar units.

Table 11.2   Cost and transition probability data ($100 units)

Age i (State)	Mean estimated repair cost	Repair limit k (Action)	Expected total cost in year $r(i, k)$ (Return)	Replacement probability $p(i, 1, k)$	Repair probability $p(i, i + 1, k)$
				(Transition probabilities)	
1	50	100	50·0	0·135	0·865
		110	48·9	0·111	0·889
		120	48·2	0·091	0·909
		130	47·8	0·074	0·926
2	75	50	87·8	0·513	0·487
		60	81·7	0·449	0·551
		70	77·0	0·393	0·607
		80	73·3	0·344	0·656
		90	70·5	0·301	0·699
		100	68·4	0·264	0·736
3		0	150·0	1·000	0·000

Solution

The problem is now in the form of the hiring a secretary problem (compare Table 10.4). The decision network is shown in Figure 11.2, where to avoid overcrowding only two actions per state have been drawn. A solution can be obtained by application of the action elimination algorithm. As this is the same in principle as Section 10.4 it will not be detailed. The Dynacode input is shown in Table 11.3, where, for brevity, only three repair limit values are shown at each state. To avoid having more than four digits in the action variables all the costs have been expressed in hundred dollar units.

Table 11.4 shows the Dynacode output. The action column gives the optimal repair limits which are 110 in state 1 and 80 in state 2. In dollar units this means that the optimal repair limit is $11,000 at age 1 and $8000 at age 2. The steady-state average cost per vehicle per year is given by the gain in Table 11.4. This is 81·475 or $8147. The optima lie away from the boundaries of the set of alternative actions so it is unnecessary to extend the set of actions searched.

It is interesting to compare the average cost figure with the corresponding cost using the economic life strategy. For the economic life method the average cost per year is given by the sum of the acquisition cost and the mean repair costs divided by the age at replacement. For replacement at various ages the costs are:

age 1 = $15,000 per year (acquisition cost only)
age 2 = (15,000 + 5000)/2 = $10,000 per year
age 3 = (15,000 + 5000 + 7500)/3 = $9166 per year

Table 11.3   Regular inspection repair limit problem: Dynacode input

```
DYNACODE REPAIR LIMITS - REGULAR INSPECTION PROBLEM
LIST INPUT
MINIMIZE
STOCHASTIC
INFINITE STAGE
TERMINAL STATES 3
STAGES 100
TOLERANCE 1.0
ZERO TERMINAL VALUES
* STATE IS AGE IN YEARS
* ACTION IS REPAIR LIMIT
* GAIN IS COST PER VEHICLE PER YEAR
* ALL COSTS ARE IN HUNDRED DOLLAR UNITS
DATA
1      1      100      50.0      0
1      1      100      0.135     1
1      1      100      0.865     2
1      1      110      48.9      0
1      1      110      0.111     1
1      1      110      0.889     2
1      1      120      48.2      0
1      1      120      0.091     1
1      1      120      0.909     2
1      2      70       77.0      0
1      2      70       0.393     1
1      2      70       0.607     3
1      2      80       73.3      0
1      2      80       0.344     1
1      2      80       0.656     3
1      2      90       70.5      0
1      2      90       0.301     1
1      2      90       0.699     3
1      3      0        150       0
1      3      0        1.0       1
END
```

Table 11.4   Regular inspection repair limit problem: Dynacode output

```
DYNACODE REPAIR LIMITS - REGULAR INSPECTION PROBLEM
* STATE IS AGE IN YEARS
* ACTION IS REPAIR LIMIT
* GAIN IS COST PER VEHICLE PER YEAR
* ALL COSTS ARE IN HUNDRED DOLLAR UNITS
*
TOLERANCE OPTIMAL POLICY
*
         STAGE          STATE          ACTION          VALUE
          18              1             110           -68.556
          18              2              80           -32.198
          18              3               0             0.000
*
          GAIN       LOWER BOUND     UPPER BOUND
         81.678        81.194          82.162
END
```

The economic life is 3 years. Comparing costs under the two strategies we have:

Economic life strategy $9166 per vehicle per year
Repair limit strategy $8147 per vehicle per year

Saving $1019 per vehicle per year

The savings in the repair limit method arise by excluding certain high cost repairs, in practice this usually means savings on high cost spares or on labour intensive repairs to old vehicles.

The transition probability data provide estimates of the proportion of vehicles replaced in each age group. With a repair limit of $11,000 the proportion of 1-year-old vehicles replaced is 0·111 or about 11%. The proportion of 2-year-old vehicles replaced with repair limit $8000 is 34%. Those figures are important for planning the purchase of replacements.

Re-sale

An assumption in the analysis so far is that vehicles whose estimated repair costs exceed the repair limit are not repaired but are scrapped as they are. It may be that such vehicles can be sold or traded in, possibly after receiving some minor repairs. In this case the average contribution (selling price — minor repairs and disposal costs) can be deducted from the acquisition costs in calculating the mean total cost per vehicle for vehicles of the given age group. Re-sale of vehicles in good repair is advantageous if the contribution received is greater than the repair limit.

11.3 Derivation of Repair Limit Formulae

In this section we derive formulae for the returns and transition probabilities needed in repair limit replacement problems. We start by considering the regular inspection problem which is solved in this chapter. To avoid subsequent repetition, we then go on to derive the formulae needed for the random failure problem discussed in Chapter 13.

Regular Inspection Problem: Probabilities of Replacement and Repair

To determine the probability of replacement for vehicles of a given age with a given repair limit we consider the distribution of estimated repair costs. Experience shows that these costs have approximately a negative exponential distribution (Figure 11.3).

The mean estimated repair cost varies with the age of the vehicle, but we can derive the key equations in terms of general values of this cost and of the repair limit. For a negative exponential distribution of estimated repair costs with mean m the probability density function is

$$f(x) = (1/m)\exp(-x/m) \tag{11.4}$$

The probability of replacement when the repair limit is k is given by the area under the repair cost distribution curve above the value of k. The area under the curve

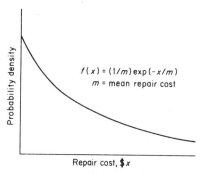

Figure 11.3   Repair costs have a negative exponential distribution

below the repair limit value gives the probability of repair. For a negative exponential distribution of estimated repair costs with mean m and for repair limit k the probabilities are shown in Figure 11.4 and are derived as follows.

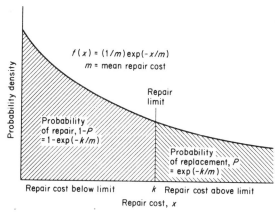

Figure 11.4   Probabilities of repair and replacement given repair limit k

The probability of replacement, P, is given by

$$P = \int_{k}^{\infty} (1/m)\exp(-x/m)\mathrm{d}x$$
$$= \exp(-k/m) \tag{11.5}$$

The probability of repair, $1 - P$, is given by

$$1 - P = 1 - \exp(-k/m) \tag{11.6}$$

Regular Inspection Problem: Costs

The mean costs incurred in the current year when a vehicle has mean estimated repair cost m and repair limit k are given by the sum of the mean cost of those repairs which are actually carried out and the mean expenditure on replacements. The mean cost of those repairs which are actually carried out is found by integration of the product of repair cost and repair probability density between zero and the repair limit, value k, thus:

$$\text{mean repair expenditure} = \int_0^k (x/m)\exp(-x/m)dx$$

$$= m[1 - (1 + k/m)\exp(-k/m)] \qquad (11.7)$$

$$= m[1 - (1 + k/m)P]$$

The mean expenditure on replacements is given by the product of the probability of replacement and the cost of replacement and is,

$$\text{mean expenditure on replacement} = AP \qquad (11.8)$$

The mean total cost in the year, denoted C, is the sum of the mean repair and replacement expenditure:

$$C = m[1 - (1 + k/m)P] + AP \qquad (11.9)$$

Equations (11.5), (11.6), and (11.9) give the decision network data thus,

$$r(i, k) = C = m[1 - (1 + k/m)P] + AP$$

$$p(i, 1, k) = P = \exp(-k/m) \qquad (11.10)$$

$$p(i, i + 1, k) = 1 - P = 1 - \exp(-k/m)$$

Random Failure Problem: Probabilities of Replacement and Survival

The random failure repair limit problem is described in Chapter 13, Section 13.2.

Consider a vehicle which enters its ith year of life. What is the probability that it will be replaced before reaching the start of its $(i + 1)$th year? To determine this we must consider how failures occur and repair costs arise.

Failure can occur at any time and there may be more than one failure per year. The failures occur as a Poisson process with rate λ failures per year. Thus, if there were no possibility of the process being terminated by replacement, the distribution of the number of failures occurring in the first year of life for the case where $\lambda = 2$ would be shown in Figure 11.5. That is the probability of zero failures would be 0·135, of 1 or 2 failures 0·271, of 3 failures 0·181, 4 failures 0·091 and so on to small probabilities of larger numbers of failures. Another property of this process is that the time between failures has a negative exponential distribution with mean $1/\lambda$.

When a failure occurs the resulting repair cost is estimated. The repair costs in a given year of life have a negative exponential distribution with mean m. The situation at any individual failure is as illustrated in Figures 11.3 and 11.4 for the regular inspection problem. Equations (11.5) and (11.6) also apply to an individual failure. Let P denote the probability of replacement at an individual failure, then by equation (11.6).

$$P = \exp(-k/m) \qquad (11.11)$$

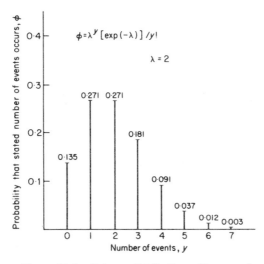

Figure 11.5   Poisson distribution with mean 2

Several failures may occur in the year, and the failure rate is λ. The replacement rate is therefore λP:

$$\text{replacement rate} = \lambda P \tag{11.12}$$

and replacement occurs as a Poisson process. The time to replacement has a negative exponential distribution with mean $1/\lambda P$ and the probability of survival for one year, denoted by S, is given by

$$S = \exp(-\lambda P) \tag{11.13}$$

The probability of replacement during the year is

$$1 - S = 1 - \exp(-\lambda P) \tag{11.14}$$

Random Failure Problem: Cost and Time

The average cost incurred per vehicle in a given age group is now derived. At each failure the average costs are the same as in the regular inspection problem and are given by the quantity C derived in equation (11.9):

$$C = m[1 - (1 + k/m)P] + AP \tag{11.15}$$

The mean number of failures in a year is given by

$$\text{mean number of failures} = \frac{\text{probability of replacement in year}}{\text{probability of replacement per failure}}$$

$$= [1 - \exp(-\lambda P)]/P \tag{11.16}$$

Hence the mean total cost per vehicle is

$$D = C[1 - \exp(-\lambda P)]P \qquad (11.17)$$

To determine the average time in service for a vehicle in a year we note that the time to replacement has a negative exponential distribution with mean $1/\lambda P$. The average service time, t, given truncation after one year is found by integrating the survival function between 0 and 1, thus

$$
\begin{aligned}
t &= \int_0^1 \exp(-\theta\lambda P)d\theta \\
&= [1 - \exp(-\lambda P)]/\lambda P
\end{aligned}
\qquad (11.18)
$$

Equations (11.13), (11.14), (11.17), and (11.18) give the decision network data thus

$$
\begin{aligned}
r(i, k) &= D = C[1 - \exp(-\lambda P)]/P \\
t(i, k) &= [1 - \exp(-\lambda P)]/\lambda P \\
p(i, 1, k) &= 1 - S = 1 - \exp(-\lambda P) \\
p(i, i + 1, k) &= S = \exp(-\lambda P)
\end{aligned}
\qquad (11.19)
$$

Vehicles which survive to the end of the last year of life are replaced, so for this year, denoted N, the cost equation becomes

$$
\begin{aligned}
r(N, k) &= D + AS \\
p(i, 1, k) &= 1
\end{aligned}
\qquad (11.20)
$$

Random Failure Problem with Discounted Returns

Let the interest rate be a. The transition probability density function for replacement is negative exponential with rate λP. The discounted transition probability is therefore

$$
\begin{aligned}
b(i, 1, k) &= \int_0^1 \lambda P \exp[-(\lambda P + a)t]dt \\
&= \lambda P\{1 - \exp[-(\lambda P + a)]\}/(\lambda P + a)
\end{aligned}
\qquad (11.21)
$$

Survivors enter state $i + 1$ at time $t = 1$. The probability of survival is $\exp(-\lambda P)$ and so the discounted survival transition probability is

$$b(i, i + 1, k) = \exp(-\lambda P + a) \qquad (11.22)$$

The cost rate at time t, given survival of a vehicle to that time, is given by

$$\text{Cost rate} = \text{average cost per failure} \times \text{failure rate} = C\lambda \qquad (11.23)$$

where C is given by equation (11.15).

The survival probability at time t is $\exp(-\lambda Pt)$ and so the present value of the mean total cost is

$$r(i, k) - \int_0^1 C\lambda \exp[-(\lambda P + a)t]dt \tag{11.24}$$

$$= C\lambda\{1 - \exp[-(\lambda P + a)]\}/(\lambda P + a)$$

In the last year of life, state N, survivors are replaced at the end of the year at cost A. The present value of the cost and the discounted transition probability are therefore given by

$$r(N, k) = AS(a) + C\lambda[1 - S(a)]/(\lambda P + a) \tag{11.25}$$

$$b(N, 1, k) = S(a) + \lambda P[1 - S(a)]/(\lambda P + a)$$

where

$$S(a) = \exp(-\lambda P + a) \tag{11.26}$$

CHAPTER 12

Markov Decision Process with Discounting

12.1 Introduction

The concepts of interest rate, discount factor, and present value were described in Chapter 3. Let the interest rate be $x\%$ per year. The present value of $\$r$ received in n years time is

$$r(1 + x/100)^n \tag{12.1}$$

Let b be the discount factor defined by

$$b = 1/(1 + x/100), \quad 0 \leqslant b < 1 \tag{12.2}$$

Suppose that a regular income of $\$r$ per year is received. The sum received in the nth year from now will have present value $b^n r$. The present value of the entire future income, denoted V, is given by

$$V = r + br + b^2r + b^3r + \ldots \tag{12.3}$$

$$= r(1 + b + b^2 + b^3 + \ldots) \tag{12.4}$$

The terms in brackets on the right-hand side of equation (12.4) form a geometric series whose sum to infinity is $1/(1 - b)$. Hence

$$V = r/(1 - b) \tag{12.5}$$

This is the limiting present value of the sequence of returns.

12.2 Markov Decision Processes with Discounted Returns

In a Markov decision process with discounted returns a system has N states labelled $i = 1, \ldots, N$. When the system visits state i an action k is chosen from a set of alternative actions. A return $r(i, k)$ is then generated and the system goes to state j with probability $p(i, j, k), j = 1, \ldots, N$. Each transition occupies a stage and future returns are discounted at interest rate $x\%$ per stage, or equivalently with discount factor b

given by equation (12.2). The maximum present value of the total return generated when the system starts in state i and continues for n stages is given by

$$f(n, i) = \text{Max} \left(r(i, k) + b \sum_{j=1}^{N} p(i, j, k) f(n - 1, j) \right) \qquad (12.6)$$

$$f(0, i) = \text{given terminal values}, \quad i = 1, \ldots, N$$

As the stage number increases the maximum present value $f(n, i)$ tends to a finite limit. This limit is analogous to the limit V given by equation (12.5), although it now involves an average over a stochastic sequence of returns. Each state has a limiting maximum present value, and for state i this is denoted $w^*(i)$. The optimal long-term policy for a Markov decision process with discounted returns is one which maximizes (or minimizes) the limiting present value of the states. A policy will exist which maximizes all the present values simultaneously. A tolerance optimal policy is one whose limiting present values all differ from the optimum by not more than a prescribed amount. Such a policy can be found by application of equation (12.6) in conjunction with bounds, a convergence test, and an action elimination test.

Bounds on the Limiting Present Values and Convergence Test

Let δ_n be the optimizing policy found at stage n and let this policy have limiting present values $w(i, \delta_n), i = 1, \ldots, N$. The bounds and convergence test for the discounted case use the value difference and error terms defined for the undiscounted case:

$$d(n, i) = f(n, i) - f(n - 1, i)$$

$$d_U(n) = \text{Max}_i \ [d(n, i)], \ d_L(n) = \text{Min}_i \ [d(n, i)] \qquad (12.7)$$

$$e(n) = d_U(n) - d_L(n)$$

However, the state values $f(n, i)$ are now present values given by equation (12.6). Expressing results of MacQueen (1966, 1967) in the current terminology, the following bounds and convergence property apply:

$$bd_L(n - 1) \leqslant d(n, i) \leqslant bd_U(n - 1) \qquad (12.8)$$

$$e(n) \leqslant be(n - 1) \qquad (12.9)$$

$$\lim_{n \to \infty} [d(n, i) = 0 \qquad (12.10)$$

for maximization, (if minimizing a corresponding result applies),

$$f(n, i) + bd_L(n)/(1 - b) \leqslant w(i, \delta_n)$$
$$\leqslant w^*(i) \leqslant f(n, i) + bd_L(n)/(1 - b) \qquad (12.11)$$

$$|w^*(i) - w(i, \delta_n)| \leqslant be(n)/(1 - b) \qquad (12.12)$$

The approximate optimal limiting present value of state i is $\hat{w}_n(i)$ given by

$$\hat{w}_n(i) = f(n, i) + \tfrac{1}{2}[b/(1-b)][d_L(n) + d_U(n)] \tag{12.13}$$

Hence the following results apply at stage n:

(1) The current policy is tolerance optimal if the right-hand side of inequality (12.12) is below the prescribed tolerance.
(2) The limiting present values of the system under a tolerance optimal policy are then $\hat{w}_n(i) \pm \tfrac{1}{2}be(n)/(1-b)$.

Action Elimination

The results of equations (10.15) to (10.18) require minor modification to allow for discounting. The value of action k at state i at stage n is now defined as,

$$f(n, i, k) = r(i, k) + b \sum_{j=1}^{N} p(i, j, k)f(n-1, j) \tag{12.14}$$

The shortfall is again

$$y(n, i, k) = |f(n, i) - f(n, i, k)| \tag{12.15}$$

but the inequality governing the reduction in shortfall is

$$y(n+1, i, k) \geqslant y(n, i, k) - be(n) \tag{12.16}$$

The action elimination test quantity $z(n, i, k)$ is as follows:

$$z(n, 1, k) = 0,$$

$$z(n, i, k) = \begin{array}{l} y(n-1, i, k) - be(n-1) \text{ if } z(n-1, i, k) \leqslant 0 \\ z(n-1, i, k) - be(n-1) \text{ if } z(n-1, i, k) > 0 \end{array} \tag{12.17}$$

for $n = 2, 3, 4 \ldots .$

Also, if

$$y(n, i, k) > be(n)/(1-b)$$

action k at state i will not pass the test at any stage after stage n.

12.3 The Repair Limit Problem with Discounting

An example of a discounted Markov decision process is the repair limit problem stated in Chapter 11, Section 11.2, but with future costs discounted at, say, 20% per annum. When Dynacode is used to solve this problem the input in Table 11.3 is modified by including the statement PERCENT 20 in the program. The output is as shown in Table 12.1.

The optimal values of the repair limit are shown in the ACTION column and are $12,000 and $9000 in years 1 and 2 respectively. These are higher than in the undiscounted case (Table 11.4), which is as one would expect, since discounting favours repair rather than replacement.

Table 12.1 shows the bounds on the limiting net present values, which for states 1, 2, and 3 in dollar units are \$45,800, \$49,500, \$53,200 approximately. Thus, if

Table 12.1 Dynacode output for the regular inspection repair limit problem with discounting

---

```
DYNACODE REPAIR LIMITS  -  REGULAR INSPECTION PROBLEM
* STATE IS AGE IN YEARS
* ACTION IS REPAIR LIMIT
* ALL COSTS ARE IN HUNDRED DOLLAR UNITS
*
TOLERANCE OPTIMAL POLICY
*
      INTEREST RATE PERCENT
        20.000
*
         STAGE           STATE         ACTION         VALUE
          16               1             120         431.273
          16               2              90         468.448
          16               3               0         505.052
*
BOUNDS ON THE NETT PRESENT VALUE
*
         STATE       LOWER BOUND     UPPER BOUND
           1           457.326         458.243
           2           494.501         495.418
           3           531.105         532.022
END
```

---

we start with a 3-year-old vehicle and apply the given tolerance optimal policy the limiting present value of future costs in a process which continues indefinitely will be \$53,200.

Economic Life Policy

Consider the application of an economic life policy with replacement at age n. The present value of the costs incurred by the first vehicle, assuming that it is purchased new initially, will be

$$G(n) = A + bc(1) + b^2c(2) + \ldots b^n c(n) \tag{12.19}$$

where A is the acquisition cost, b is the discount factor and $c(i)$ is the mean cost incurred at age i (reduced to a present value at the start of the year). For the regular inspection repair limit problem with discounting at 20% interest rate equation (12.19) gives, for replacement at age 3 and working in \$100 units,

$$G(3) = 150 + 0 \cdot 833 \times 50 + (0 \cdot 833)^2 \times 75 = 243 \cdot 69$$

For an infinite planning horizon the cost $G(n)$ is incurred at n year intervals with effective discount factor b^n, so that the limiting present values of future costs is W given by

$$W = G(n)/(1 - b^n) \qquad (12.20)$$

In the example

$$W = G(3)/(1 - b^3) = (243 \cdot 69)/(1 - 0 \cdot 578$$

$$= 577 \cdot 464$$

In dollar units the present value of future costs is \$57,700 approximately. This figure can be compared with the cost under the optimal repair limit policy:

Economic life policy	\$57,700
Repair limit policy	\$53,200
	Saving \$4500

The present value of the savings achieved by the repair limit policy at 20% interest rate is \$6800.

CHAPTER 13

Semi-Markov Decision Processes

13.1 Data Transformation

The Markov decision problems considered in Chapters 10 to 12 had stages of equal duration. In this chapter we consider systems where the mean durations of visits to each state may vary with the state visited and the action chosen. The aim is to find a policy which maximizes (or minimizes) the average return generated per unit time. Problems with this structure are called semi-Markov decision problems. The name arises from the fact that under any policy the system follows a Markov process if it is observed only at the times of entry to a new state. These are also called Markov renewal processes. The 'time' parameter can be generalized to any type of stage variable and may be continuous or discrete.

Semi-Markov decision problems can be solved by applying a transformation to the data (Schweitzer 1971). The transformation creates an ordinary Markov decision problem whose gain per stage under any policy is the same as the gain per unit time of the original problem. This transformation is now described.

In the original (semi-Markov) problem, for action k in state i let the associated return be $r(i, k)$, the mean duration of the visit to the state be $t(i, k)$ and the probability of transition to state j be $p(i, j, k), j = 1, \ldots, N$. The data transformation technique requires that the time scale be chosen so that

$$t(i, k) \geqslant 1 - p(i, i, k) \tag{13.1}$$

The transformed (Markov) data are $r'(i, k), p'(i, j, k)$ given by

$$r'(i, k) = r(i, k)/t(i, k) \tag{13.2}$$

$$p'(i, j, k) = p(i, j, k)/t(i, k) + \delta_{ij}[1 - 1/t(i, k)]$$

where

$$\delta_{ij} = 0 \text{ if } i \neq j, \delta_{ii} = 1.$$

169

Once this transformation has been applied the semi-Markov problem can be solved as an ordinary Markov decision problem. The Schweitzer transformation is summarized in Table 13.1.

Table 13.1   The Schweitzer transformation

	Untransformed (semi-Markov)	Transformed (Markov)
Return	$r(i, k)$	$r(i, k)/t(i, k)$
Time	$t(i, k)$	—
Transition probability	$p(i, j, k)$	$p(i, j, k)/t(i, k) + \delta_{ij}[1 - 1/t(i, k)]$

13.2 Random Failure Repair Limit Problem

An example of a semi-Markov decision process is a repair limit replacement problem in which failure and the associated repair/replacement decision can occur at any time. The following is based on the Land Rover replacement problem described by Hastings (1970).

Problem Statement

A vehicle costs 400 money units when new and can last for up to two years. During its first year of life failures occur as a Poisson process with mean two failures per year and during its second year of life as a Poisson process with mean three failures per year. When failure occurs the cost of the repair which is required is estimated. The estimated repair costs have a negative exponential distribution with mean 100 money units in the first year and mean 150 money units in the second year. The times between failures and the repair costs are assumed to be stochastically independent. The estimated repair cost is compared with a repair limit. If the repair limit is exceeded the repair is not carried out and the vehicle is replaced. Otherwise the repair is carried out and the vehicle continues in service. Vehicles which survive to the end of the second year of life are always replaced. The aim is to determine repair limits for vehicles in each year of life which minimize the expected average cost of repairs and replacements per unit time.

Formulation

A vehicle can be in either its first year of life, state $i = 1$, or in its second year of life, state $i = 2$. The action variable is the repair limit k. As in the regular inspection problem of Chapter 10 it is only necessary to consider a few discrete values of the repair limit for each age group. The return $r(i, k)$ is the mean total repair and replacement expenditure on a vehicle in year of life i given repair limit k. The time $t(i, k)$ is the mean amount of service which a vehicle provides from the start of its ith year of life until it leaves that age group. A vehicle may leave an age group either because it survives a full year and therefore enters year of life $i + 1$ or

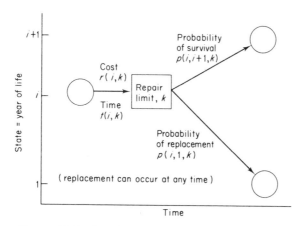

Figure 13.1   Random failure repair limit problem:
network components

because it is replaced during the year. Because replacement can occur at any time
$t(i, k)$ will be less than one year. The transition probabilities are the probability of
replacement $p(i, 1, k)$ and of survival into the next year of life $p(i, i + 1, k)$. The
components of the decision network formulation are illustrated in Figure 13.1.
The decision network is shown in Figure 13.2. Vehicles which reach the age limit
are replaced, so replacement is inevitable for vehicles in the second year of life.

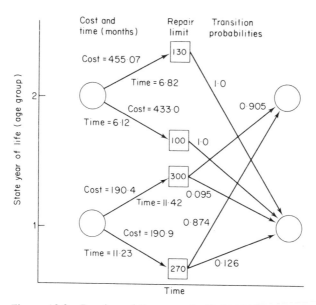

Figure 13.2   Random failure repair limit problem: the
decision network

172

Data Calculations

The costs, times, and transition probabilities for the random failure repair limit problem are derived in Chapter 11, Section 11.3, and are given in equations (11.19) and (11.20).

Table 13.2(a) BASIC program for repair limit data calculations: random failure problem

```
1∂    REMARK REPAIR LIMIT RANDOM FAILURE DATA CALCULATIONS
2∂    READ A
3∂    PRINT "ACQUISITION COST"A
4∂    READ M
5∂    PRINT "MEAN REPAIR COST"M
6∂    READ L
7∂    PRINT "FAILURE RATE    "L
8∂    PRINT
9∂    READ N
1∂∂   PRINT "LIMIT","COST","TIME","P.REPLACE","P.SURVIVE"
11∂   FOR I=1 TO N
12∂   READ K
13∂   P=EXP(-K/M)
14∂   S=EXP(-P*L)
15∂   R=M*(1-P*(1+K/M))
16∂   D=(R/P+A)*(1-S)
17∂   T=(1-S)/(P*L)
18∂   PRINT K,D,12*T,1-S,S
19∂   NEXT I
2∂∂   REMARK REPLACEMENT COST
21∂   DATA 4∂∂
22∂   REMARK MEAN ESTIMATED REPAIR COST
23∂   DATA 1∂∂
24∂   REMARK FAILURE RATE PER YEAR
25∂   DATA 2
26∂   REMARK NO. OF REPAIR LIMITS, REPAIR LIMITS,...
27∂   DATA 5,27∂,28∂,29∂,3∂∂,31∂
28∂   END
```

Table 13.2(b) Results from running the program shown in Table 13.2(a)

```
ACQUISITION COST 4∂∂
MEAN REPAIR COST 1∂∂
FAILURE RATE     2
```

LIMIT	COST	TIME	P.REPLACE	P.SURVIVE
27∂	19∂.915	11.2285	.125769	.874231
28∂	19∂.6∂6	11.299	.114515	.885485
29∂	19∂.43	11.3633	.1∂42∂7	.895793
3∂∂	19∂.365	11.4219	9.47771E-∂2	.9∂5223
31∂	19∂.393	11.4753	8.61585E-∂2	.913841

DONE

Notes: In the last year of life the survivors are replaced. The replacement probability is then 1 and the cost is increased by the product of the acquisition cost and the replacement probability. The modified cost can be output by changing D to $A*S + D$ in line 180 of the program given in Table 13.2(a).

As in the regular inspection case we estimate an initial set of repair limits using linear depreciation. The cost of a new vehicle is 400 and the maximum life is two years. The repair limit for each year of life can be approximated by the depreciated value half way through the year, giving values of 300 for year 1 and 100 for year 2. As in Chapter 11, we can use a short computer program to calculate the decision network data. A suitable BASIC program is shown in Table 13.2(a) and the results from a run of this program are in Table 13.2(b).

The program has been used to generate data for the following range of repair limits:

Year of life 1	Repair limits	270, 280, 290, 300, 310	
Year of life 2	Repair limits	100, 110, 120, 130, 140	

The data for these actions are summarized in Table 13.3. The average service times have been expressed in months rather than years. All the times are greater than one month and this ensures that inequality (13.1) will be satisfied, so that the Schweitzer transformation can be applied.

Solution

Application of the Schweitzer transformation to the data of Table 13.3 will give a standard Markov decision problem which can be solved by the action elimination algorithm. If Dynacode is used it will accept the data in semi-Markov form and carry out the transformation internally. A semi-Markov formulation is indicated by including the statement SEMI MARKOV in the program. The time associated with each action is inserted in a time statement which immediately follows the return statement for the action. The semi-Markov data records for an action are illustrated in Figure 13.3. Table 13.4 shows the Dynacode input for the random failure repair limit problem.

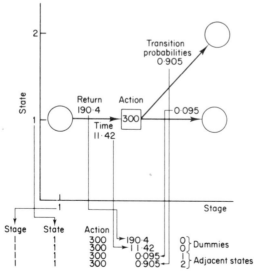

Figure 13.3   Decision network to Dynacode data:
semi-Markov action

Table 13.3   Cost, time, and transition probability data for the random failure repair limit problem

Year of life, i	Failure rate, λ	Mean estimated repair cost, m	repair limit, k	Mean total cost $r(i, k)$	Mean service time (months) $t(i, k)$	Probability of replacement $p(i, 1, k)$	Probability of survival $p(i, i+1, k)$
(state)			(action)	(return)	(time)	(transition probabilities)	
1	2	100	270	190·9	11·23	0·126	0·874
			280	190·6	11·30	0·115	0·885
			290	190·4	11·36	0·104	0·896
			300	190·4	11·42	0·095	0·905
			310	190·4	11·48	0·086	0·914
2	3	150	100	433·1	6·12	1·0	0·0
			110	439·9	6·36	1·0	0·0
			120	447·3	6·59	1·0	0·0
			130	455·1	6·82	1·0	0·0
			140	463·3	7·05	1·0	0·0

Table 13.4   Random failure repair limit problem: Dynacode input

```
DYNACODE RANDOM FAILURE REPAIR LIMIT PROBLEM - DECISION NETWORKS
LIST INPUT
MINIMIZE
STOCHASTIC
SEMI MARKOV
TERMINAL STATES 2
STAGES 100
ZERO TERMINAL VALUES
TOLERANCE 0.5
* STATE IS YEAR OF LIFE
* ACTION IS REPAIR LIMIT
* GAIN IS AVERAGE COST PER VEHICLE PER MONTH
DATA
1      1      270      190.9      0
1      1      270      11.23      0
1      1      270      0.126      1
1      1      270      0.874      2
1      1      280      190.6      0
1      1      280      11.30      0
1      1      280      0.115      1
1      1      280      0.885      2
1      1      290      190.4      0
1      1      290      11.36      0
1      1      290      0.104      1
1      1      290      0.896      2
1      1      300      190.4      0
1      1      300      11.42      0
1      1      300      0.095      1
1      1      300      0.905      2
1      1      310      190.4      0
1      1      310      11.48      0
1      1      310      0.086      1
1      1      310      0.914      2
1      2      100      433.1      0
1      2      100      6.12       0
1      2      100      1.0        1
1      2      110      439.9      0
1      2      110      6.36       0
1      2      110      1.0        1
1      2      120      447.3      0
1      2      120      6.59       0
1      2      120      1.0        1
1      2      130      455.1      0
1      2      130      6.82       0
1      2      130      1.0        1
1      2      140      463.3      0
1      2      140      7.05       0
1      2      140      1.0        1
END
```

Results

The Dynacode output is shown in Table 13.5. The tolerance optimal repair limits
are 280 in the first year of life and 130 in the second year of life. The average cost
per vehicle per year under this policy is 34·276 per month or 411·3 per year. The
optimal economic life policy is replacement at age 2 which gives a cost of 525

Table 13.5   Random failure repair limit problem: Dynacode output

---

```
DYNACODE RANDOM FAILURE REPAIR LIMIT PROBLEM - DECISION NETWORKS
* STATE IS YEAR OF LIFE
* ACTION IS REPAIR LIMIT
* GAIN IS AVERAGE COST PER VEHICLE PER MONTH
*
TOLERANCE OPTIMAL POLICY
*
```

STAGE	STATE	ACTION	VALUE
20	1	280	-220.260
20	2	130	0.000

*

GAIN	LOWER BOUND	UPPER BOUND
34.290	34.086	34.494

END

Notes: The tolerance optimal repair limits are 280 in the first year of life and 130 in the second year
of life. The average cost per vehicle per month is 34·29 or 411·5 per year.

units per year. The saving of the repair limit policy is 113·7 units per year or
21·7%.

13.3 Semi-Markov Decision Processes with Discounting

In this section we consider semi-Markov decision processes in which returns are
continuously discounted at interest rate α.

When returns are continuously discounted at interest rate α per unit time the
present value of a sum r received after time t is $r \exp(-\alpha t)$. Suppose that a system
enters state i at time $t = 0$ and that an action k is chosen. The system then makes
a transition to state j at time t with probability density $\phi_{ijk}(t)$, $j = 1, \ldots, N$. Let
$S_{ik}(t)$ be the probability that the system remains in state i for time t or longer,
given action k. If the system is still in state i at time t it generates returns at rate
$r_{ik}(t)$. The mean present value at time $t = 0$ of the return generated at the visit to
state i is denoted $r(i, k)$ and given by

$$r(i, k) = \int_0^\infty S_{ik}(t) \, r_{ik}(t) \exp(-\alpha t) \, dt \tag{13.3}$$

Let $f(n, i)$ be the maximum mean present value of the total return generated over n
transitions by a system which starts by entering state i. The following recurrence
relation holds:

$$f(n, i) = \underset{k}{\text{Max}} \left(r(i, k) + \sum_{j=1}^{N} \int_0^\infty \phi_{ijk}(t) \exp(-\alpha t) f(n-1, j) \, dt \right) \tag{13.4}$$

Let $b(i, j, k)$ be defined by

$$b(i, j, k) = \int_0^\infty \phi_{ijk}(t) \exp(-\alpha t) \, dt \tag{13.5}$$

$b(i, j, k)$ is the discounted transition probability from state i to state j under action k. The sum of the terms $b(i, j, k)$ over all states j will be less than one.

Using definition (13.5), equation (13.4) can be re-written as

$$f(n, i) = \underset{k}{\text{Max}} \left(r(i, k) + \sum_{j=1}^{N} b(i, j, k) f(n - 1, j) \right) \qquad (13.6)$$

The Laplace transform of a function $f(t)$ is

$$\int_0^\infty f(t) \exp(-at)\, dt$$

Thus $r(i, k)$ and $b(i, j, k)$ are respectively the Laplace transforms of the functions $[S_{ik}(t) r_{ik}(t)]$ and $\phi_{ijk}(t)$.

Equation (13.6) differs from the recurrence relation of an ordinary discounted Markov decision process (equation (12.6)) only in that the sums over j of the elements $b(i, j, k)$ vary with the state and action.

The present values of the states tend to the same limit as the planning horizon recedes, regardless of whether one considers the time remaining as tending to infinity or the number of transitions remaining as tending to infinity. Computationally it is simpler to let the number of transitions tend to infinity, and hence the stage variable, n, is the number of transitions remaining in the planning period. The limiting optimal present value of state i is $w^*(i)$ given by

$$w^*(i) = \lim_{n \to \infty} f(n, i) \qquad (13.7)$$

where $f(n, i)$ is the value of state i at stage n, given by equation (13.6).

The determination of a tolerance optimal policy by the action elimination algorithm follows a procedure which is similar in principle to that used in the discrete time problems of Chapter 12, but with modifications of detail caused by the unequal sums of the $b(i, j, k)$ terms over $j = 1, \ldots, N$. The Schweitzer transformation is not required for the discounted case.

13.4 Random Failure Repair Limit Problem with Discounted Costs

The random failure repair limit problem was described at the start of Section 13.2.

The decision network components are shown in Figure 13.4. As in the undiscounted case, the state variable, i, is the year of life. A stage is a transition, involving either survival for a complete year and entry to the next age group, or replacement during the year. Vehicles which survive to the ultimate life (two years in the example) are replaced. The return is now the discounted cost for a given age group, that is the cost expressed as present value at the time of entry into that age group. This varies with the age group i and repair limit k and is denoted $r(i, k)$. The discounted transition probabilities of replacement and survival are denoted

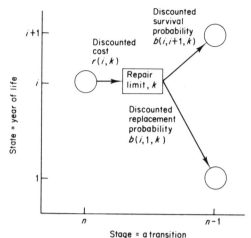

Figure 13.4 Random failure repair limit
problem with discounted returns: network
components

$b(i, 1, k)$ and $b(i, i + 1, k)$. These are derived in Chapter 11, Section 11.3, and the formulae are given in equations (11.21) to (11.25).

A BASIC program for calculating the discounted returns and discounted transition probabilities is shown in Table 13.6, and results obtained from this program are shown in Table 13.7. Table 13.8 summarizes the data for the relevant range of failure rate, repair cost, and repair limit values. The decision network is shown in Figure 13.5, the Dynacode input in Table 13.9, and the output in Table 13.10.

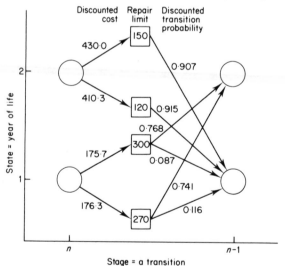

Figure 13.5 Random failure repair limit problem with
discounted returns: the decision network (only two actions per state are shown)

Table 13.6   BASIC program for repair limit data calculations: random failure problem with discounting

```
1Ø    REMARK REPAIR LIMIT RANDOM FAILURE DATA DISCOUNTED
2Ø    READ A
3Ø    PRINT "ACQUISITION COST"A
4Ø    READ M
5Ø    PRINT "MEAN REPAIR COST"M
6Ø    READ L
7Ø    PRINT "FAILURE RATE    "L
8Ø    READ X
9Ø    PRINT "INTEREST PERCENT"X
1ØØ   PRINT
11Ø   READ N
12Ø   PRINT "REPAIR","DISCOUNTED","DISCOUNTED","DISCOUNTED"
13Ø   PRINT "LIMIT","COST","P.REPLACE","P.SURVIVE"
14Ø   FOR I=1 TO N
15Ø   READ K
16Ø   P=EXP(-K/M)
17Ø   Y=-((L*P)+(X/1ØØ))
18Ø   S=EXP(Y)
19Ø   Q=(L*P)*(S-1)/Y
2ØØ   R=M*(1-P*(1+K/M))
21Ø   C=R+A*P
22Ø   D=(C*L)*(S-1)/Y
23Ø   PRINT K,D,Q,S
24Ø   NEXT I
25Ø   REMARK REPLACEMENT COST
26Ø   DATA 4ØØ
27Ø   REMARK MEAN ESTIMATED REPAIR COST
28Ø   DATA 1ØØ
29Ø   REMARK FAILURE RATE PER YEAR
3ØØ   DATA 2
31Ø   REMARK INTEREST RATE PERCENT
32Ø   DATA 16.5
33Ø   REMARK NO. OF REPAIR LIMITS, REPAIR LIMITS,...
34Ø   DATA 5,27Ø,28Ø,29Ø,3ØØ,31Ø
35Ø   END
```

Note: For the last year of life change statement 230 to PRINT $K, D + A*S, S + Q$

Table 13.7   Results from running the program shown in Table 13.6

```
ACQUISITION COST 4ØØ
MEAN REPAIR COST 1ØØ
FAILURE RATE     2
INTEREST PERCENT 16.5
```

REPAIR LIMIT	DISCOUNTED COST	DISCOUNTED P.REPLACE	DISCOUNTED P.SURVIVE
27Ø	176.321	.116155	.741255
28Ø	176.Ø36	.1Ø5743	.75Ø797
29Ø	175.815	9.62Ø96E-Ø2	.759537
3ØØ	175.729	8.749Ø5E-Ø2	.767533
31Ø	175.732	7.95243E-Ø2	.77484

Table 13.8 Discounted costs and transition probabilities

Year of life, i	Failure rate, λ	Mean estimated repair cost, m	Repair limit, k	Discounted mean cost $r(i, k)$	Discounted probabilities of:	
					Replacement $b(i, 1, k)$	Survival $b(i, i+1, k)$
(state)			(action)	(return)	(transition probabilities)	
1	2	100	270	176·3	0·116	0·741
			280	176·0	0·106	0·751
			290	175·8	0·096	0·760
			300	175·7	0·087	0·768
			310	175·7	0·080	0·775
2	3	150	120	410·3	0·915	
			130	416·5	0·912	
			140	423·0	0·909	
			150	430·0	0·907	
			160	437·3	0·904	

Interest rate $16\frac{1}{4}\%$ per annum.

Table 13.9   Random failure repair limit problem with discounting: Dynacode input

---

```
DYNACODE RANDOM FAILURE REPAIR LIMIT PROBLEM - DISCOUNTED COSTS
LIST INPUT
MINIMIZE
STOCHASTIC
SEMI MARKOV
TERMINAL STATES 2
STAGES 100
ZERO TERMINAL VALUES
TOLERANCE 1.0
PERCENT 16.5
* STATE IS YEAR OF LIFE
* ACTION IS REPAIR LIMIT
DATA
1       1       270     176.3    0
1       1       270     0.116    1
1       1       270     0.741    2
1       1       280     176.0    0
1       1       280     0.106    1
1       1       280     0.751    2
1       1       290     175.8    0
1       1       290     0.096    1
1       1       290     0.760    2
1       1       300     175.7    0
1       1       300     0.087    1
1       1       300     0.768    2
1       1       310     175.7    0
1       1       310     0.080    1
1       1       310     0.775    2
1       2       120     410.3    0
1       2       120     0.915    1
1       2       130     416.5    0
1       2       130     0.912    1
1       2       140     423.0    0
1       2       140     0.909    1
1       2       150     430.0    0
1       2       150     0.907    1
1       2       160     437.3    0
1       2       160     0.904    1
END
```

The optimal values of the repair limit are 270 in year 1 and 140 in year 2. The limiting present values of future costs are 2327 if we start with a new vehicle and 2538 if we start with a 1-year-old vehicle. The former cost excludes the cost of the new vehicle and if this added (at cost 400) the limiting present value is 2727.

The optimal economic life policy is to replace at age 2. The limiting present value for this policy is calculated using the continuous time equivalent of equation (12.20). The repair costs in each year must be expressed as present values at the start of the year. Since the repair limits are now infinite equation (11.23) reduces to

$$r(i, \infty) = (m\lambda/a)[1 - \exp(-a)] \tag{13.8}$$

Table 13.10   Random failure repair limit problem with discounting: Dynacode output

```
DYNACODE RANDOM FAILURE REPAIR LIMIT PROBLEM - DISCOUNTED COSTS
* STATE IS YEAR OF LIFE
* ACTION IS REPAIR LIMIT
*
TOLERANCE OPTIMAL POLICY
*
      INTEREST RATE PERCENT
         16.499
*
         STAGE              STATE          ACTION           VALUE
          74                  1              270          2327.127
          74                  2              140          2538.333
*
BOUNDS ON THE NETT PRESENT VALUE
*
         STATE      LOWER BOUND     UPPER BOUND
           1          2327.291        2327.437
           2          2538.497        2538.643
END
```

Note: The tolerance optimal repair limits are 270 in the first year of life and 140 in the second year
of life.

and equation (11.22) reduces to

$$b = \exp(-a) \tag{13.9}$$

For $a = 0.165$ we have

$$\exp(-a) = 0.852, \ 1 - \exp(-a) = 0.148, \ [1 - \exp(-a)]/a = 0.914$$

Hence the limiting present value under an economic life policy is given by

$$W = \frac{400 + 100 \times 2 \times 0.914 + 0.852\,(150 \times 3 \times 0.914)}{1 - 0.852^2}$$

$$= 3410$$

Comparing costs under the economic life and repair limit policies we have

	Limiting present value of costs
Economic life policy	3410
Repair limit policy	2727
Saving	683

The repair limit policy gives a saving of 683 units in the present value of future
costs.

CHAPTER 14

Further Computational Aspects and Applications

14.1 Summary of Dynacode

General

Dynacode is a computer software package for decision network calculations. To use the system the problem in hand is first put into a decision network formulation. This is converted into computer input and run on the Dynacode package. The results appear in a standard format, subject to some broad choices available to the user. The system is structured to the decision network method and provides guidance to the user on the principles involved. It has diagnostic tests which reduce the risk of formulation errors. For larger problems, Dynacode has built-in file handling facilities which are used automatically as required. The system is also valuable as an instruction medium.

Availability

The Dynacode system can be implemented on most types of computer with 32K or more words of core storage, file handling facilities, and a Fortran compiler. Terms of availability for installation on the user's computer system are available from Mr G. W. Morgan, Albany Interactive Ltd, 6 Church Street, Bromsgrove, West Midlands, England. This company also offers a service for running individual problems and supporting consultancy.

Program Statements

A Dynacode program consists of several statements selected from the list below which indicate the structure of the current problem. Each statement is entered on a separate input record (e.g., a punched card or file record). Entries normally start in column 1 but leading blanks are allowed. Some columns of the input record may be reserved for a user's sequence number, dependent on the installation. The complete list of Dynacode program statements is as follows. A summary of the vocabulary is given in Table 14.1.

DYNACODE heading

All Dynacode programs start with this statement. The heading can consist of any alphanumeric characters specified by the user. The statement will be output as the first line of the input and output.

LIST INPUT

If this statement is used it must be the second statement in the program (that is, immediately after the statement DYNACODE). It causes the program and data to be listed.

* title statement

A statement which starts with a * is a title statement. The statement can contain any alphanumeric characters specified by the user. The title statements (if any) are output before the numeric results. These statements are usually used to describe the stage, state and action variables and to summarize the problem formulation.

MINIMIZE

Indicates a minimization problem; if this statement does not appear maximization is assumed.

TERMINAL STATES m

This statement must appear. m is a positive integer which gives the number of terminal states in the problem.

RANK k

When this statement is used the system outputs a table giving the k best actions at each state, assuming that optimal actions are used at subsequent states. k is a positive integer not exceeding 25.

PERCENT x

This statement indicates that future returns are to be discounted at interest rate x per stage or per unit time (SEMI MARKOV problems). x is a positive real number. $x \geqslant 0 \cdot 1$ in INFINITE STAGE or SEMI MARKOV problems. Dynacode calculates the discount factor from the given interest rate.

STATIONARY

This statement means that the data are the same at every stage. When it is used the data for stages after the first are not entered. INFINITE STAGE and SEMI

MARKOV problems are assumed to be stationary whether or not this statement appears.

STAGES n

This statement is necessary in STATIONARY, INFINITE STAGE, and SEMI MARKOV problems. If the problem is finite stage then n is the limiting number of stages which the system operates. In INFINITE STAGE or SEMI MARKOV problems n is the limiting number of stages which are to be computed, unless convergence occurs earlier. n is a positive integer not exceeding 9999.

INITIAL STATE i

This statement may be used in deterministic problems except those which are INFINITE STAGE. i is the label of an initial state. When this statement appears the optimal process from state i only is printed. Otherwise, the optimal process from every initial state is printed.

STOCHASTIC

This statement means that the decision network has stochastic transitions and that a stochastic data format will be used. If it is omitted deterministic data are assumed.

INFINITE STAGE
SEMI MARKOV

At most one of these statements may appear. INFINITE STAGE means that the system has a discrete and invariant index parameter (e.g., equal discrete time intervals) and that a steady-state or limiting solution is required. SEMI MARKOV means that the index parameter is continuous and/or varies with the state or action, and that a steady-state or limiting solution is required. If neither of these statements appears then a finite stage problem is assumed.

PROGRESSIVE

This statement means that the network has a progressive structure. PROGRESSIVE problems cannot be STATIONARY, INFINITE STAGE or SEMI MARKOV.

ZERO TERMINAL VALUES

This statement is only valid in STATIONARY, INFINITE STAGE or SEMI MARKOV problems. When used it sets the values of the terminal states to zero. Otherwise the values of the terminal states are supplied as data.

TOLERANCE y

This statement is used in INFINITE STAGE or SEMI MARKOV problems. y is a positive real number and is the difference between the upper and lower bounds on the gain or limiting present values, below which computation stops. It controls the degree of convergence in these problems, subject to the possibly overriding control of the statement STAGES n. If this statement is omitted the compiler sets $y = 0$.

DATA

This statement announces that the data are about to start.

END

END indicates that the data are finished.

Data Statements

General Rules

Dynacode data consist of a series of records, each of which contains five numbers, separated by one or more blanks or by commas. When punched card input is used, each card contains one record, and similarly when file input is used each file record contains one input record.

The first three numbers in each input record are stage, state, and action labels which are always integers in the range -9999 to 9999. The fourth number is a real number (integer or decimal) and may be the value of a terminal state, a return, a time or a transition probability depending on the context. This real number can be up to eleven characters in length, inclusive of minus sign and decimal point, if any. The fifth number is the label of an adjacent state and is always an integer in the range indicated earlier in this paragraph. Blanks in an input record are not interpreted as zeros. The five numerical entries are said to occupy five fields, referred to as the *stage, state, action, real,* and *adjacent state* fields. Every field must always contain a numeric entry, and where a field is not strictly relevant a dummy entry, usually a zero, is inserted.

Terminal Values

The data start with entries indicating the values of the terminal states unless the statement ZERO TERMINAL VALUES appears in the program. There is an input record for each terminal state. The stage field contains the stage label of the terminal stage; the state field contains the label of the current state; the action field is not strictly relevant and contains a dummy entry, usually a zero; the real field contains the value of the current state; finally the adjacent state field is not relevant and contains a dummy entry, usually a zero. Thus each entry is of the form

$$n, i, 0, v, 0$$

where

$$n = \text{terminal stage variable}$$
$$i = \text{terminal state variable}$$
$$0 = \text{dummy entry (zero)}$$
$$v = \text{terminal state value}$$
$$0 = \text{dummy entry (zero)}$$

Deterministic Action Data

There is an input record for each action arrow in deterministic networks. The sequence of these records must be the same as when the data are used in the backward pass of the calculation procedure. For each action the data record contains the entries

$$n, i, k, r, j$$

where

$n = $ stage variable of the start node of the action
$i = $ state variable of the start node of the action
$k = $ action variable
$r = $ return associated with the action
$j = $ adjacent state, that is, the state variable of the end node of the action

Stochastic Action Data

The data for each action in a STOCHASTIC problem consist of a set of records, comprising a return record and one or more transition probability records. The first record in the set is the return record. This gives the return associated with the action and has the form

$$n, i, k, r, 0$$

where

$$n = \text{stage variable of the start node of the action}$$
$$i = \text{state variable of the start node of the action}$$
$$k = \text{action variable}$$
$$r = \text{return associated with the action}$$
$$0 = \text{dummy entry (zero)}$$

There is a transition probability record for each adjacent state which is accessible from the current state with probability $p > 0$. No transition probability record is needed for states reached with probability zero.

The transition probability records have the form

$$n, i, k, p, j$$

where

    n = stage variable of the start node of the action
    i = state variable of the start node of the action
    k = action variable
    p = transition probability to adjacent state j, $0 < p \leqslant 1$
    j = adjacent state variable

Note that it is permissible for the transition probability to take the value 1. When it does there will be a single transition probability record with entries of the form n, i, k, 1, j; where j is the adjacent state reached with probability one.

The transition probabilities for each action must sum to unity. In discounted SEMI MARKOV problems p is a discounted transition probability and in this case the sum of the discounted transition probabilities for each action must not exceed 0·99. For SEMI MARKOV problems with undiscounted returns see also the next section.

Semi-Markov Undiscounted Action Data

The action data for SEMI MARKOV undiscounted problems is similar to that for other STOCHASTIC problems but with the addition of a *time record* which appears immediately after the return record for each action, and before the transition probability records. The time record entries have the form

$$n, i, k, t, 0$$

where

    n = stage variable of the start node of the action
    i = state variable of the start node of the action
    k = action variable
    t = time associated with the action
    0 = dummy entry (zero)

Other Points

In PROGRESSIVE problems the stage variable is zero for terminal states, 1 for intermediate states and 2 for initial states.

In STATIONARY, INFINITE STAGE, and SEMI MARKOV problems the stage variable is zero for terminal states and 1 for the states at stage 1. The data for subsequent states is not entered.

Output

The results from Dynacode appear in the form of tables with a standard layout. If errors are made on input, self-explanatory error messages are printed.

14.2 Summary of Applications

A summary of applications of the decision network method is given in Table 14.2.

Table 14.1 Summary of Dynacode vocabulary

Statement	Default setting or notes
DYNACODE heading	essential
LIST INPUT	input not listed if omitted
MINIMIZE	maximize if omitted
STOCHASTIC	deterministic if omitted
STATIONARY	nonstationary if omitted
INFINITE STAGE or	
SEMI MARKOV	finite stage is omitted
PROGRESSIVE	serial (stagewise) if omitted
TERMINAL STATES m	essential. m = number of elements in the set of terminal states
ZERO TERMINAL VALUES	optional for STATIONARY problems, invalid otherwise
STAGES n	essential for STATIONARY problems
INITIAL STATE i	i = initial state variable, deterministic finite stage problems only
PERCENT x	x = interest rate per stage, discounted problems only
TOLERANCE y	INFINITE STAGE or SEMI MARKOV only
RANK k	optional
* comment statement	optional
DATA	essential
$n, i, 0, v, 0$	stage, state, dummy, terminal value, dummy (omit if ZERO TERMINAL VALUES)
....	
n, i, k, r, j	stage, state, action, return, adjacent state⎫ deterministic
or	
$n, i, k, r, 0$	stage, state, action, return, dummy
n, i, k, p, j	stage, state, action, transition probability, adjacent state⎫ STOCHASTIC
or	
$n, i, k, r, 0$	stage, state, action, return, dummy
$n, i, k, t, 0$	stage, state, action, time, dummy
n, i, k, p, j	stage, state, action, transition probability, adjacent state⎫ SEMI MARKOV
....	
END	essential

Table 14.2 Applications of decision networks

Area	State	Action	Return
Sequential planning			
inventory	stock level	order quantity	income from sales, stockholding costs, ordering costs
production	stock level	production quantity	income from sales, production costs
production capacity	capacity level	increase or decrease capacity	income from sales, production costs, plant purchase costs
transport fleet capacity	capacity level	purchase quantity	cost of new items, hire charges
replacement	age of item	replace, repair, overhaul	replacement costs, repair costs
reservoirs	water level	release quantity	irrigation, pollution control
manpower planning	workforce level	hire, fire, re-deploy wage level	wages, overtime, redundancy costs, training costs, social benefits and disbenefits
medical care	state of health	type of treatment, e.g., hospitalization or home care	cost of treatment, value to patient and others
queueing and machine interference	queue length	service policy, repair pool size	waiting time and costs, service costs
Routing			
roads, tracks, transmission lines, tunnels	geographical position	direction from current point	construction cost
production process routeing	set of completed operations	next operation	production cost
Allocation			
volume in containers	volume remaining	item loaded	transport costs
advertising budget	money remaining	allocation to a product	income from sales
resource depletion	resources remaining	amount used now	income or benefits from use of resource
money to projects	money remaining	allocation of money to a particular project	yield from project
Trimloss			
steel buying	sizes required	size purchased	purchase costs
cutting	sizes required	cutting decision	trimloss
standardization of sizes	sizes required	sizes produced as standard	trim costs, production costs

References and Bibliography

Bellman, R. E. (1957). *Dynamic Programming*, Princeton University Press, Princeton, NJ.

Clark, J. A. and Hastings, N. A. J. (1977). 'Decision networks'. *Operational Res. Q.*, **28**, 51–68.

Hastings, N. A. J. (1970). 'Equipment replacement and the repair limit method'. In A. K. S. Jardine (Ed.), *Operational Research in Maintenance,* Manchester University Press, Manchester.

Hastings, N. A. J. (1971). 'Bounds on the gain of a Markov decision process'. *Operations Res.*, **19**, 240–4.

Hastings, N. A. J. (1973). *Dynamic Programming with Management Applications,* Butterworths, London and Crane-Russak, New York.

Hastings, N. A. J. (1976). 'A test for nonoptimal actions in undiscounted finite Markov decision chains'. *Manmt Sci. (Theory)*, **23**, 87–92.

Hastings, N. A. J. *Dynacode Decision Network/Dynamic Programming Software System Handbook.* G. W. Morgan, Albany Interactive Ltd, 6 Church Street, Bromsgrove, England.

Hastings, N. A. J. and Mello, J. M. C. (1973). 'Tests for suboptimal actions in discounted Markov programming'. *Manmt Sci. (Theory)*, **19**, 1019–22.

Hastings, N. A. J. and van Nunen, J. (1977). 'The action elimination algorithm for Markov decision processes'. Department of Mathematics, Eindhoven University of Technology, The Netherlands.

Howard, R. A. (1960). *Dynamic Programming and Markov Processes*, Wiley, New York.

Howard, R. A. (1971). *Dynamic Probabilistic Systems*, Wiley, New York.

Jardine, A. K. S. (1973). *Maintenance, Replacement and Reliability*, Pitman/Wiley, London/New York.

Lockyer, K. G. (1969). *An Introduction to Critical Path Analysis*, Pitman, London.

MacQueen, J. (1966). 'A modified dynamic programming algorithm for Markovian decision processes'. *J. Math. Analysis Applic.*, **14**, 38–43.

MacQueen, J. (1967). 'A test for suboptimal actions in Markovian decision problems'. *Operations Res.*, **15**, 559–61.

Mahon, B. H. and Bailey, R. J. M. (1975). 'A proposed improved replacement policy for Army vehicles'. *Operational Res. Q.*, **26**, 477–94.

Mine, H. and Osaki, S. (1970). *Markovian Decision Processes*, Elsevier, Amsterdam.

Mitchell, G. H. (1972). *Operational Research*, English Universities Press, London.

Moder, J. J. and Phillips, C. R. (1970). *Project Management with CPM and PERT*, Van Nostrand Reinhold, New York.

Odoni, A. R. (1969). 'On finding the maximal gain of a Markov decision process'.

Operations Res., **17**, 857–60.

Porteus, E. L. (1971). 'Some bounds for discounted sequential decision processes'. *Manmt Sci.,* **18**, 7–11.

Roberts, S. M. (1964). *Dynamic Programming in Chemical Engineering and Process Control,* Academic Press, New York.

Schweitzer, P. J. (1965). 'Research in control of complex systems', Technical Report No 15, Operations Research Centre, Massachussetts Institute of Technology.

Schweitzer, P. J. (1971). 'Iterative solution of the functional equations of undiscounted Markov renewal programming'. *J. Math. Analysis Applic.,* **34**, 495–501.

Schweitzer, P. J. and Federgruen, A. (1976). 'The asymptotic behaviour of undiscounted value iteration in Markov decision problems'. Mathematical Centre, 2e Boerhaavestraat, Amsterdam, The Netherlands.

Su, S. Y. and Deininger, R. A. (1972). 'Generalization of White's method of successive approximations to periodic Markovian decision processes'. *Operations Res.,* **20**, 318–26.

Index

193